DAVE MEURER

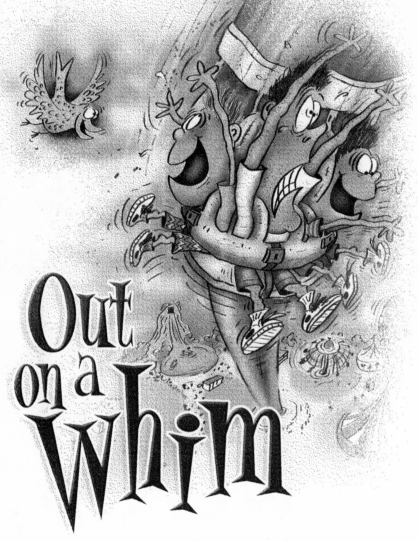

Out on a Whim

BETHANYHOUSE
MINNEAPOLIS, MINNESOTA

Published by Bethany House Publishers
A Ministry of Bethany Fellowship International
11400 Hampshire Avenue South
Bloomington, Minnesota 55438

Printed in the United States of America

ISBN 0-7394-1962-5

To the many teachers
who had a hand in teaching me the craft of writing,
refused to accept sloppy work,
encouraged me to write,
and went above and beyond the call of duty.
Special thanks to Eldridge Trott for all the above,
but also for going out of your way
to set me up for success.
(You know what I mean.)
Bless you.

DAVE MEURER works for the United States House of Representatives as an aide to a California congressman. He is the winner of numerous state and national writing awards and honors. His writings have appeared in major publications, including *Focus on the Family* and *Homelife*. The Meurer family lives in northern California.

Dave Meurer can be reached at Meurerdaze@aol.com or by writing to Bethany House Publishers, 11400 Hampshire Ave. So., Bloomington, MN 55438.

Acknowledgments

All book projects that finally make it onto the shelves are ultimately the result of a group effort, so there is certainly enough blame to go around for everyone involved in this one. I only *wrote* this thing, so no one can pin all the responsibility on me.

The first person I am going to implicate is my editor, Steve Laube. This is the *third time* he has agreed to publish my stuff, so he cannot plausibly claim ignorance. I think we would all understand one little mistake, and perhaps even chalk the second one up to inexperience or mental illness or a concussion. But *three* times? Steve is clearly culpable here.

I next point the accusatory finger at all the other people at Bethany House Publishers—people like Holly Foster, Elizabeth Anderson, Jeanne Mikkelson, Melissa Smith, and even The Carol. Each of these persons should be considered unindicted coconspirators, as all of them played a role.

Tragically, even the widely respected editor of *Focus on the Family* magazine, Tom Neven, has fostered my writing career (even going so far as to insert my material into Dr.

Dobson's otherwise respectable publication).

Doug Newton of *Light & Life* magazine also bears considerable guilt, as he is the first editor of a Christian publication to print my stuff. Thousands of Free Methodists will never be the same, including poor Margie.

Chip Macgregor, my hyperactive and semi-lunatic agent, made no attempt to halt this project. And he used to be a *minister*! You just have to shake your head.

Additionally, not a single member of my family lifted a finger to stop me—not Dale, the beloved wife of my youth, not my two boys, Mark and Brad, and not even my mom and dad. If this does not come under the heading of "contributing to the delinquency of an author," then I don't know what does.

Lastly, I have friends, co-workers, and even *church people* who provided winks and nods and occasionally even Chee-tos. If I am hauled into court, I'm naming names.

Contents

Preface 11

How to Get the Most Out of This Book 15

Section 1: *Wholly Unrelated Topics*

1. What Would Rambo Do? 19
2. Pause for Concern 23
3. Good-bye, Obadiah! 29
4. Virtual Christianity 35
5. The Most Terrifying Danger of All 39

Section 2: *Totally Random Observations*

6. Of Prose and Pills 49
7. "Does This Guy Get PAID for Blathering About
   NOTHING?" 55
8. Sort of Unsolved Mysteries 59
9. Without a Prayer 67
10. Out With the Old 73

Section 3: *Various and Sundry Mutterings*

11. Cry "Uncle!" 81

12. Soul Music.. 93

13. College Daze....................................101

14. Fishing Diary 107

15. Under the Influence............................113

Section 4: *"Other"*

16. Flammable Household Appliances (and Other
    Combustible Close Calls).......................119

17. We, the Genders 127

18. If You Can't Say Something Nice, You Still May
    Need to Say It 135

19. The Mysterious Man...........................141

20. Church People 147

21. The Uncivil War 151

22. What Dave Would Tell You If He Was a Minister
    and You Accidentally Allowed Him Into Your Pulpit
    One Day..159

23. Grate Expectations 171

24. It All Depends 183

Preface

"*Out on a Whim?* What kind of title is that? Just what, *exactly*, is this book about?" you may be wondering, which means that you are asking *precisely* the question my editor kept asking. Is this an interesting coincidence, or what?

I just hope that you have a whole lot more patience than my editor. As the months wore on and the big yellow bulldozer of time kept pushing us inexorably toward the sheer cliff of the deadline, he became increasingly agitated.

"Just have faith," I would advise him.

"What is *that* supposed to mean?" he would snap.

Faith is something we are all supposed to have. It says so right in the Bible. You'd think that a so-called "Christian editor" would already understand this very basic aspect of his belief system.

"Just give me a general idea of where you are going with the book," he would grouse into the phone. "We need to get some ad copy for the catalog."

"By faith Abraham went forth, even though he did not know where he was going," I would reply. "That's a story right out of the Bible. Wasn't Abraham a wonderful example?"

"TELL ME WHAT THE BOOK IS ABOUT OR I'LL GRAB YOUR SPLEEN AND . . ."

I was compelled to hang up on him several times, so shrill was his hysteria. When I had agreed, months earlier, to do yet another book, I never dreamed that my editor would demonstrate such volatile behavior as the project moved into its final phases.

One day, after ignoring his sixteen increasingly antagonistic e-mail messages, I received a phone call at three o'clock in the morning.

"I'm begging," he whispered. "I stuck my neck out and offered you a contract nine months ago. Like a FOOL, I trusted you to behave like a professional. Now I've got the production people breathing down my neck every day; the marketing people are actually throwing desk implements at me, and I have broken out in a nervous rash on my left nostril. P-l-e-a-s-e, just give me a hint about the content, and don't you DARE lecture me again about my lack of faith. Editors don't *do* faith!"

"Steve, Steve, Steve," I muttered groggily, but with compassion. "O ye of little . . ."

WHAM!

Telephone poles actually quivered, so hard did he slam down the phone.

Preface

I am sure you will agree that since my own editor did not get a synopsis of this book, it would hardly be fair for me to offer a sneak peek to you.

So just dive in. And have some faith.

How to Get the Most Out of This Book

This volume is divided into four sections in order to help you grasp the logical progression of ideas:

Section One: Wholly Unrelated Topics

Section Two: Totally Random Observations

Section Three: Various and Sundry Mutterings

Section Four: "Other"

Different readers will use this book in a variety of ways.

Sunday School Teachers will find that habitually un-involved, easily bored junior high students will show a new attentiveness if you wave this book in their faces in a threatening manner while shouting at them. They won't actually learn anything, but sometimes we have to snatch what little victories we can. You may wish to have a Polaroid camera on hand too so you can record the moment and impress their parents.

Pastors will be pleased to discover that their worst and most disjointed sermons suddenly seem brilliant and insightful when compared to these chapters. So buy a few hundred copies for your congregation and watch them suddenly appreciate you more.

Scholars and **Seminary Students** utilizing this book should be ashamed of themselves.

At the end of each chapter is a **Study Guide** that **Small Groups** can use if they have way too much time on their hands.

Section 1

Wholly Unrelated
Topics

Chapter 1

What Would Rambo Do?

It has become commonplace in recent years for church youth group kids to ask themselves, "What would Jesus do?" about a given situation, such as the neighbor's yappy little poodle coming into your yard each morning to perform its daily doodle. Inevitably, the answer to the WWJD question turns out to be something selfless and kind and thoughtful. While I certainly applaud these young people for asking this probing question, I think it is informative, by way of contrast, to ask what *other* significant people, such as Rambo, would do.

For example, in the aforementioned scenario, the answer would clearly be "Lock and load and blow the poodle away." But since this is clearly not what Jesus would have done, we can learn that this is something we must avoid even though it is *extremely* tempting.

Or we could wonder, "What would Takamiyama (the

famous champion Sumo wrestler) do?" Hint: the tiny canine would be a lot flatter.

"What would Richard Nixon do?" Order the IRS to audit the poodle owners.

"What would NASA do?" Launch the poodle into space, thus scientifically proving that it is, technically, possible to rid the planet of these pests one poodle at a time, and at only six times the original budget projections.

Broadening the cast of decision makers, we may wish to probe, "What would Congress do?" The answer, obviously, is that they would have a sharp and acrimonious debate, and Republicans would draft popular legislation offering tax breaks to anyone who bought a beagle while the Democrats charged that this risky scheme would harm America's children.

"What would President Clinton have done if he were still in office which, thank God, he is not?" Proposed free diapers for all poodles. The Senate would have ridiculed that proposal until they saw polling figures indicating that a whopping 72 percent of swing voters agreed with the president's statement that "we must solve the poodle diaper funding crisis." Ultimately, both measures would have died in committee and the Senate would recess for the month of August.

Clearly, there is a deep moral lesson here. And that lesson is, um, if you were reading your Bible right now instead of my material, you wouldn't be wasting valuable time. You would also know a lot more about what Jesus would do because you could read what He already did and thereby get a pretty good clue.

Study Guide Questions

1. **Question for men:** Deep down, haven't you always wanted to try target practicing with a grenade launcher or a bazooka? Me too.

2. **Discuss with group:** If I could legally own a tank for one day, the target I would most like to practice on is _____. (NOTE: If the answer is something like "Fi-Fi" or "Muffy," you really need to reread the chapter.)

3. What IS IT with guys that makes us want to blow things up?

4. Aren't you just AMAZED when you consider the massive amount of firepower at Jesus' disposal—which he *never* used even on people who really, really, *really* deserved it? Me too.

‖ Chapter ‖ 2

Pause for Concern

Solve the Mystery: An ill-fated family of four is stranded in a car on a country road in South Dakota during the worst blizzard of the century. One person has numb toes, one person's teeth are chattering, one person is shivering, and one person is fanning herself and saying, "Gracious, it is so *hot* in here."

QUESTION: Which one is experiencing menopause?

HINT: If you answer correctly, you may get whacked with a spatula.

I had never even heard the word *menopause* when it decided to pay my mom a nice little visit (in the sense that a forest fire pays Yellowstone a nice little visit). I came home from school one day and walked in the door and said, "Hi, Mom," and she erupted in a geyser of tears, collapsed on the sofa, and sobbed, "Go ahead, just rub it in!"

I turned quizzically to my dad, who was wildly making the universal gesture for "Meet me in Ohio!"

Dad drove me across four county lines before he cleared his throat and announced, "Your mother is going through 'The Change.'"

"The change of what?" I asked.

Dad bit his lip.

"Son, there comes a time in every woman's life when her body decides that her child-bearing days are over. Her hormones are in a state of upheaval, and it is exhibited in moodiness, hot flashes, tears, and the ability to rip the doors off a Brinks armored truck if chocolate is inside. Just try to be understanding."

That directive turned out to be easier said than done.

The term "try to be understanding" implies that there is something that can, in fact, be understood—like algebra or mathematical word problems, which at least involve logic. Menopause is more complex than quantum physics, and no rules of logic apply.

EXAMPLE: If Menopausal Woman "A" is driving west at 35 miles per hour, and Menopausal Woman "B" is driving east at 65 miles per hour, and both of them forget why they even got in their cars, so they drive to Baskin Robbins and happen to arrive at the same time and each consume a triple scoop cone of Chocolate Rampage with Almonds and then start commiserating about water retention and how no one even *tries* to understand them and they are NOT cooking dinner tonight and if he really loved her he would take her out to the Italian Cottage Restaurant for lasagna, how come when they get home they are mad at the kids?

Although it will still be several years before The Change descends on our house like an asteroid smashing into Nebraska,* the Meurer household is already in training for this momentous event. We hold monthly drills called PMS, which is sort of like training for a National Guard exercise, except it is more dangerous and we don't even get free uniforms.

Women believe it is tremendously unfair that they have to endure PMS, childbirth, *and* menopause, because they think men pretty much get off scot-free. But they are mistaken. While it is true that women have to do the labor thing, the childbirth thing, and endure the cramps, aches, pains, water retention, bloating, hot flashes, sudden fits of weeping, hormone-driven maniacal mood swings, and embarrassing OB/GYN exams, they need to bear in mind that guys have to *live in the same house with them* while all this is happening. So we males are certainly shouldering our share of the suffering. Hey, I think you could even argue that guys are doing *most* of the heavy lifting, because sometimes we even have to go to the store late at night to buy Midol for our womenfolk.

WHACK, WHACK, WHACK!!! OW, OW, OW!!!

---

*Which could actually increase property values, as there would finally be *something* interesting to look at.

(Sound of a spatula smacking the elbow of a completely unarmed writer.)

You may recall that in the biblical account wherein God told Abraham that the pitter-patter of little feet would soon be heard around the tent, Sarah, who was nearly 100 years old, laughed. While the text tells us it was a laugh of unbelief, we can conjecture that one component of this unbelief may have taken the form of Sarah thinking to herself, "*Surely* the Lord would not make me go through menopause TWICE?!? I can't *believe* it!"

Be that as it may, the happy couple did get a baby out of the ordeal—it's just that half of the happy couple was a bit happier than the other, and had less stretch marks.

But it is all a package deal. The entire PMS/pregnancy/menopause thing is a wondrously orchestrated system God has created so that we can bring children into the world to nurture and teach and then release into adulthood to start the amazing process all over again—with menopause serving as an "off" switch so that women finally get a break and do not have kids at age 100 unless God is really trying to make a major point.

Although we don't understand why much of this has to be kind of an unpleasant experience for women, we need to trust that in the grace and goodness of God, there is, in fact, a reason for it. At minimum, we can be thankful that, except for those late-night Midol runs, men pretty much get to skate. Works for me!

WHACK, WHACK, WHACK!!! OW, OW, OW!!!

Study Guide Questions

1. **Question for guys:** If you had your choice regarding what kitchen implement you were going to get whacked with by an emotional menopausal woman, you would choose:
   - (a.) spatula
   - (b.) basting bulb
   - (c.) garlic press
   - (d.) refrigerator

2. What makes you think you'll have a *choice?*

3. A weepy, hormone-intensive woman mostly needs:
   - (a.) love and understanding
   - (b.) help around the house
   - (c.) dinner out
   - (d.) chocolate
   - (e.) all of the above, but start with the chocolate before someone gets hurt.

Chapter 3

Good-bye, Obadiah!

Several years ago the Reader's Digest company created quite a stir when it published a "condensed" version of the Bible, marketing it as *The Same Venerable Bible You Have Always Known and Loved, but With All the Boring Parts Taken Out.*

Well, they didn't come right out and say it that way, but they implied it.

Many people were aghast and incensed that someone would try to edit the Bible. Not me! I thought it was a *stellar* idea. My only complaint is that the Reader's Digest people didn't go far enough. While they took out all the dull stuff about who begat whom, they left in *wads* of material I would prefer to skip.

Specifically, I wish they would have omitted the parts that tell me to

- give money to other people;
- pray for people I don't like;
- forgive little weasel-breath ingrates who don't deserve it; and
- pay taxes.

There is nothing quite so irritating as picking up a Bible to get a little dose of inspiration and accidentally winding up in the Sermon on the Mount, where we are told to "bless those who persecute you."

While the Psalms are usually a pretty good bet for something uplifting and poetically appealing, even they are fraught with the real danger of finding commands to go do something you would prefer not to do. Personally, I prefer certain "begat" passages over some of the Psalms, because at least the genealogies don't get pushy.

Speaking of pushy, you can pretty much ignore the book of James if you are looking for something upbeat and unmeddlesome. Romans has some good stuff in the uplifting department, but it is mostly in chapter eight and you have to wade through a bunch of theology to get there.

What we need is a carefully edited "all inspiration, all the time" Bible that offers us all the positive and affirming material and leaves out the preachy stuff.

I attempted to do exactly that, but you'd be surprised at just how much of the Bible is devoted to changing us into something other than what we already are. I mean, you can barely get past a few pages before there is some kind of moral lesson or command to do something other than what you are already doing or are planning to do.

Happily, I have discovered that, with careful editing, you can extract oodles of positive words and link them together to create festive, encouraging messages that are still, technically, "right out of the Bible." For example, meticulous editing of the following completely unrelated passages can yield a perky, positive "verse of the day." Just pull out the **bolded** words and see what I mean.

"If you had responded to my rebuke, I would **have** poured out my heart to you and made my thoughts known to you" (Proverbs 1:23).

"**A** mocker resents correction; he will not consult the wise" (Proverbs 15:12).

"**Happy** are those who do not follow the advice of the wicked" (Psalm 1:1 NRSV).

"I warn everyone who hears the words of the prophecy of this book: If anyone adds anything to them, God will add to him the plagues described in this book. And if anyone takes words away from this book of prophecy, God will take away from him his share in the tree of **life** and in the holy city, which are described in this book" (Revelation 22:18–19).

Yes, the affirming message "Have a happy life" can be cobbled together from a series of passages that could otherwise be sort of heavy and judgmental. And even *more* editorial flexibility can be achieved if we edit individual *letters* out of words. That way, we can come up with "biblical" messages that can literally say anything we want them to say, and we don't have to go through the laborious process of searching through a bunch of passages that may contain disturbingly confrontational, non-uplifting themes.

As it says in the Bible (once you link together a bunch of letters from Philippians), "You deserve a break today."

Study Guide Questions

1. Have you ever even read the book of Obadiah?

2. If "no," then why are you all pushed out of shape at the Reader's Digest people? It's not exactly skin off your nose.

Chapter 4

Virtual Christianity

The British news service, Reuters, ran a story not too long ago titled "Don't Fire, Just Say, 'Bang.'" Here is an actual excerpt from the story:

British Royal Navy recruits are being ordered not to fire live shells. Instead they are instructed to shout, "Bang!" It is all part of a Ministry of Defense drive to save money, but sailors say it makes a mockery of their training.

"It's like being a kid again, playing cowboys and Indians in the school ground," one recruit said, according to media reports of the novel instructions.

"It is a sad joke, and sailors are disgusted. It makes you ask what the navy is coming to," he said.

The instructions were issued to sailors at the gunnery school in Plymouth, southwest England.

They check coordinates, line up a target, and prepare to fire the shells, which cost 642 pounds each.* Then they shout, "Bang!"

---

*A little less if they go on Weight Watchers.

"This is part of the Armed Forces' continuing efforts to achieve the best possible value for money," a spokesman told Saturday's *Daily Telegraph*.

This newspaper account was sent to me by a friend who thought the Brits have really sort of gone down the tubes since Margaret Thatcher left #10 Downing Street. But I think our English friends are on to something. If they take this cost-cutting a step further, we could be reading news reports that go like this:

LONDON (Rooters) In an effort to conserve paper, Parliament today agreed to cease writing down any new laws, opting instead to just try to remember what measures they pass.

"Parliament enacts approximately 3,000 measures per year, and recording it all is depleting our forest resources," said Sir Uppington Blithe. "Entire groves of trees went down just to print the paper for the legislation mandating the reduction of excessive paperwork."

However, acrimony has already erupted as various measures have been recalled differently by Members of the Parliament.

"I distinctly recall passage of a tax reduction last week, but my esteemed colleague on the other side of the aisle insists that it was actually the Commemoration of Bread Pudding Week," said Sir Horatio Bowlgirth of Shrubbery.

The two officials came to fisticuffs over the incident.

In related budgetary news, the Queen agreed to reduce the cost of her staggeringly expensive wardrobe.

"She actually looks rather peppy in a jogging suit," said her spokesperson.

Far from ridiculing our British friends, I think we could learn a grand lesson on frugality. For example, I notice that a significant portion of many church budgets is consumed by sending missionaries to distant, expensive destinations in steamy little third world nations that feature terribly overgrown foliage. It can cost THOUSANDS of dollars just for the airfare, not to mention the 467 cans of RAID bug spray.

Imagine the cost savings if we implemented a "virtual missionary" program in which we went down to the local garden shop and purchased scores of exotic plants and created a little jungle in the church parking lot.

(The skeptics and traditionalists will argue that you can't truly replicate a missionary venture without a target population of uncivilized people who dress in bizarre clothing and engage in strange rituals. Fortunately, most high school youth groups fill that bill quite nicely, so you probably have that base covered. We just need some bait to lure them into the shrubbery so the missionaries can look for them. I think Hostess HoHos will do the trick.)

So let us thank our commonsense British buddies for showing us the way.

After all, as Lord Wilberforce Stublet of Mince put it so well so many years ago, "If a thing is worth doing, it is worth not doing at all."

Study Guide Questions

1. Why do the British call their currency a "pound" when they could have just as easily called it a "ton"?

2. Can you believe that the author did NOT make up that story about the British Navy? It is an actual news item. His editor sent it to him. His editor wastes huge amounts of time reading weird, useless stuff, which is how this book ended up in print. So the author is certainly not going to lodge a formal complaint.

3. If you were heading up the Missions Committee in your church, what kind of foliage would you favor for the church parking lot jungle? (NOTE: The author is partial to hydrangeas.)

4. Why are otherwise rational adult persons willing to go be missionaries in distant nations that in many cases are both dangerous and have terrible TV reception?

Chapter 5

The Most Terrifying Danger of All

They were hiding under the blankets, not daring to even peek at me.

I was at the most scary part of the story.

The mysterious creature was hard on the heels of the two brave little boys as they dashed up the cold stone steps of the castle tower. They dared not look behind them.

Would the brave boys free the imprisoned prince, or would they fall into the clutches of the scary, unseen creature they could hear pounding up the stairs behind them?

Most little boys enjoy the thrill of being scared—but not *too* scared. It is a fine line for a dad to walk.

Let's take adventure stories, for example. If the plot is too tame, you lose their interest and they complain and ask for a brand-new story, and you have kissed off twenty minutes of the pre-bedtime ritual.

But a truly scary story is fraught with its own problems. If you get the kids too frightened, to the point where they jump at every sound or can't go to sleep or develop nervous facial tics or have a complete emotional breakdown and require years of expensive treatment at a specialty clinic in Zurich, then your wife may get mad at you.

Theme parks invest millions of dollars in research and development to strike that delicate balance between "exciting" and "raw screaming terror plus a lawsuit." But parents don't typically have access to those kinds of resources. So we just have to wing it and look for subtle clues, like the kids falling asleep (a nonverbal clue meaning: *"This story is boring."*) or the kids turning white and fainting and requiring the services of paramedics (a nonverbal clue meaning: *"Boy, is Dad in trouble with Mom again!"*)

Fortunately, I struck a good balance early on with my boys. When they were little guys, about four and six years old, I developed a surefire formula that combined the fear of the unknown with the comforting assurance of a tale that always ended exactly the same. (This is not a novel approach, and certainly not one for which I would claim credit. If you were unfortunate enough to have grown up watching the absolutely PATHETIC science fiction program called *Lost in Space*, you saw the *same plot* 267 times: Space ship piloted by hapless family and fake-looking

robot almost makes it home to earth, only to be foiled
again by the stupid and greedy Dr. Smith.)*

This is how my story formula would work:

The tale would always be about two brave little boys
named Mark and Brad, who went on some kind of adventure, such as a trek through the dark woods or a submarine
expedition. There would always be hints of Someone, or
Something, watching and following them. Toward the
very end of this gripping narrative, the Someone or Something would be slowly closing in on the brave little boys,
who were TRAPPED and could not get away.

It was at that point that their tiny little hands would
be clutching the covers and little eyes would be peering
from beneath the blankets.

Then came the clincher.

"Then, Mark and Brad saw something huge," I would
say. "Something terrifying. Something dangerous. It was
so terrifying and so dangerous that many people would say
it was the most terrifying danger of ALL!"

That line was always *precisely* the same.

At this point they would scramble out from beneath
the blankets and grab their most powerful weapons, their
pillows, and shout in unison, "You better not say it!"

---

*I *despised* Dr. Smith. The only reason I kept watching this irritating show—
other than the fact that it was on—was because I was sure that sooner or later
they would eject him right into space, or vaporize him, or at *least* give him a
Charley horse and I didn't want to miss it when it happened. As it turns out,
the entire space family was too *stupid* to realize this was an option. No wonder they kept floundering around from planet to planet. They deserved it.

"Say what?" I would ask in startled innocence.

"We know what you are going to say and you better not or me and Brad will smack you with pillows!" Mark would say.

"Yeah!" Brad would add.

"Oh, I know what you're thinking," I would say. "But this time it is going to be different, so you better get back under the blankets!"

They would dive for cover.

"But you better not do it!" Mark would caution.

I would ignore him and continue the story.

"It was huge. It was frightening. It was 250 feet tall!"

The boys were tensed—coiled like over-tight springs—ready to pounce on me in a millisecond, but not willing to risk being out from the protective cover of the comforter on the infinitesimally slim chance that the story would end differently this time.

"It came right at them," I continued.

Pause.

"It was a gigantic, enormous, terrifying . . . BARBIE DOLL! It was a *BARBADON*!"

They would bolt from beneath the covers at lightning speed, delivering a hail of unrelenting pillow assaults.

"That wasn't scary!" Brad would shout, body-slamming himself on top of me like a very tiny member of the U.S. National Wrestling Team.

The attack would last seven or eight minutes, until

they were worn out and I surrendered.

"You have to tell us a REAL scary story tomorrow," Mark would insist as I tucked them into bed.

But the next night would be pretty much like the night before. My job was to make things exciting, but safe in the end.

As time wore on, scary stories sort of faded away. I don't remember the day. There just came a time when they were too old for bedtime stories. But the desire for an exciting thrill never fades away for a boy. Thus several years later the Meurer family found itself at a theme park, seated in a horrifyingly tall ride called "The Drop Zone," our feet dangling out in space as we looked way, way down at people the size of hydrogen molecules.

The Drop Zone didn't look all that tall from the ground. But sitting up in the stratosphere, I realized this was completely irresponsible of me. I sensed that Mark and Brad were sitting there in raw fear—too scared to even move—desperately trying not to lose bladder control. I looked around in vain for an intercom or some way to communicate with ground control in order to beg mercy for my terrified kids. But there was nothing but miles of air.

For those of you who are unfamiliar with The Drop Zone, picture yourself strapped into a sofa that has been lashed to the top of a twenty-seven-story telephone pole. They haul you to the top and then drop you in a free fall.

Air brakes are supposed to bring you to a halt at the bottom, and the "fail safe" is that if the air brakes don't work, you'll be too flat to sue.

I felt wracked with guilt at what I was putting my boys through. I knew the fear had to be almost overwhelming.

"Isn't this COOL?" Brad exclaimed.

"Awesome!" answered Mark.

"WE'RE GOING TO DIE!" I shrieked.

"Dave, will you please stop screaming that?" Dale whispered sharply. "After all, it's just a ride!"

It took nineteen hours to rise to a height roughly twice that of Mt. Everest. Then they dumped us like ballast from a hot air balloon.

"Wah-hoo!" shouted Brad.

"Yeah!" echoed Mark.

"AIIIIEEEEEEEEEE!!" I screeched as we plunged toward the earth at warp factor nine.

I awoke to the sensation of someone gently slapping my face.

"Are you all right, sir?" asked a young woman dressed in a theme park uniform.

"I can't *believe* he fainted," Brad was grousing.

"Fainted?" I retorted, struggling to my feet. "I was just resting. The ride was a snoozer. I dozed off."

"Wanna go again?" Mark asked eagerly.

"Your father has had enough 'rest' for one day," Dale commented dryly.

The kids ran back to get in line while two smirking assistants wheeled me to a park bench and gave me a cold compress.

I have been scared a *lot* since then. But not of insane rides, which I will not go on again until people start surfing in the Sahara.

Rather, it is life outside the amusement park that truly scares me—whether my boys are learning to ride horses, rafting down the Klamath River with the youth group, snow skiing down runs that would freeze-dry my liver, dealing with tough kids at school, or making important life choices—all while I outwardly try to act serene and unruffled as I quietly bite my lip and pray like mad for them. Because parenthood is the scariest ride you can climb aboard. It doesn't seem like that big of a deal when you are looking at it from the ground, before you actually strap in. But it is huge. It is frightening. It is 250 feet tall. It can be so terrifying and so dangerous that sometimes it seems like the most terrifying danger of all.

And you can't get back in line for another turn. Furthermore, unlike my adventuresome bedtime stories, there is no guarantee of a safe and happy ending.

I think parenthood is the ultimate "Drop Zone."

Sometimes it is so scary that all we can do is close our eyes and hold on to the hand of God as he whispers, *"Do not fear, for I am with you"* (Isaiah 41:10).

That is infinitely more security than air brakes.

Study Guide Questions

1. Since Dr. Smith is just a fictional character in the discontinued *Lost in Space* television series, is it OK, as a Christian, to hate his guts? Discuss in a small group setting after watching several episodes.

2. How come our kids grow up so fast? One day you are tucking them into bed and telling them exciting stories, and suddenly they are in high school and you are talking about career choices and you realize that they will soon be gone and nothing will ever be the same. Do you ever get kind of emotional about this?

3. Me too.

Section 2

Totally
Random
observations

Chapter 6

Of Prose and Pills

Some people get really outraged about the cost of prescription drugs, especially after they find out that the chemical content may total mere pennies for pills that retail for several dollars apiece. But what these incensed people often do not realize is that the pharmaceutical companies spend hundreds of millions of dollars researching and then abandoning drugs that did not pan out.

Likewise, authors can expend massive amounts of time and reams of paper working on book ideas that never pay off. You, the reader, end up holding one of the few projects that made it through the grueling approval process.

For instance, this is my third book to make it to the bookshelves. But I have dozens of proposed titles that were summarily rejected, such as:

- *Methodist Biker Chick Confessions: The Saga of Seven Activist Sunday School Teachers Who Cruise Into Rural Alabama*

Towns and Force the Southern Baptists to Study the Writings of John Wesley
- *Dynamic Church Gossip*
- *Touched by an Anglican*
- *Enraged Episcopalians and the Congregations Who Love Them*
- *King James Is the Only Version of the Bible Personally Approved by God, Which Is Kind of a Bummer for the French*
- *Blending the Skim Milk of Duty With the Captain Crunch of Joy*
- *Flannelgraphs and Pepper Spray: Bringing New Focus to Rowdy Sunday School Classes*
- *Ten Quick Tips to Squelch Small Group Communication: If You Wanted THEIR Opinion, You Would Have Asked for It*
- *Children of a Lesser Presbyterian*

and my all-time favorite,
- *Traumatic Lessons From the Mission Field: I Wish Someone Would Have Told Me That "Indigenous" Is Just a Fancy Word for "Naked"*

Any one of these titles could have *and should have* been a smashing success, but each one was blown out of the sky like an ill-fated duck on the opening day of the season—the tattered feathers of prose drifting slowly into the muddy pond of rejection as trigger-happy editors give each other the high-five of self-congratulatory glee.

Here is how the process works:

An author pours his heart and soul into a writing project. Many authors have worked for years—some have worked their entire adult lives—on *one* manuscript. These authors harbor a vision wherein a thoughtful, serious, literate editorial professional slowly savors the manuscript over a cup of Earl Grey tea late at night in a quiet, book-lined study. These authors are not so much harboring a vision as they are harboring a hallucination.

In reality, their manuscript is merely one of several jillion on the way to a publishing house that is already so swamped with unsolicited manuscripts that there is no possible way the editors have time to read yet one more. So in a secret agreement that the naïve author would never dream possible, the manuscript is quietly rerouted to a pharmaceutical company where it is read by underpaid laboratory rats.

These are not happy rats, either. These are surly, perturbed, overworked rodents who daily face the prospect of ingesting yet another experimental medication that has a slim chance of curing cancer but which, more likely than not, will cause them to grow another head which, just to add insult to injury, is a dead ringer for Sam Donaldson. Plus, they have terrible health insurance plans and zero stock options. So we are talking about a *tough* audience. It is amazing that *any* books get published at all.

When the hapless author gets his manuscript back, it

is covered in harsh red marks that he assumes are editorial comments but which are completely unintelligible and look suspiciously like rat tracks.

It is so incredibly difficult to get a book published that, statistically, it *never* happens. So you should seriously consider the possibility that you are not reading a book at all right now, but are merely suffering from a hallucination brought on by ingesting a flawed pharmaceutical product that somehow slipped through the FDA approval process.

If you suddenly find Sam Donaldson looking over your shoulder, you may want to ask him to do an exposé on TV.

Study Guide Questions

1. Suppose for some reason you HAD to grow a second head. Would it make you feel any better if it looked like Ted Koppel? (Women, please substitute "Barbara Walters.")

2. Some people object to experiments on laboratory animals, including rats, even if this research produces life-saving new drugs for human use. Many of these people see no difference between taking the life of an animal and taking the life of a human. You probably do not want to invite these people over to a barbecue unless you are grilling celery.

3. Discuss with your group the theological flaws apparent in the thinking of the aforementioned group. Also discuss how you can barbecue pork without having it get too dry, but also get it done enough to not come down with scurvy or measles or whatever scary thing you get from ingesting undercooked pork. Please send your answers to me. I'm doing ribs for a big party. Thanks!

Chapter 7

"Does This Guy Get PAID for Blathering About NOTHING?"

At this point, some readers will be scratching their heads and muttering, "That last chapter was very *odd*. There appears to be no overarching moral or biblical lesson in it. How can this be a so-called 'Christian book' if it has entire chapters that don't convey any specifically Christian content?"

I am glad they are asking that question, because it provides me an opportunity to reply, "Would you *please* lighten up?"

Here's the key question: Was it funny? C'mon, admit it. When you got to the part about laboratory rats, didn't you kind of giggle—or at least smile? And if so, is there anything *wrong* with that?

Can Christian people enjoy humor for humor's sake?

Or art for art's sake? Or tea for the sake of having tea, without pouring it out of a hugely overpriced "Christian" pot that has a Bible verse plastered on it?

Don't get me wrong. I embrace the concept of making an actual point through a story. I do it all the time. I believe in the power of a parable—which was Jesus' primary way of communicating truth. He was a teller of tales—stories of lost sheep, lost coins, and lost sons. He gave us great, memorable stories about the pearl of great price and the kind Samaritan. But He undoubtedly also said things that had no apparent moral point to them, such as, "Could you pass the salt, please?"

And the salt shaker, or whatever they used back then to hold salt, was not purchased at a Christian bookstore and thus it did not have "Ye are the salt of the world" written on it in tiny cursive letters.

The Faith does not have to be plastered on, and crammed into, everything in sight. I would love to see a Christian bookstore sell some really great art that does not have a Bible verse printed on it, just to convey the message that we believe in beauty—and we don't feel like it has to somehow be "justified" by slapping a psalm on it.

I have a friend named Steve who used to manage a Christian bookstore that featured not only books and Bibles but also all kinds of toys and objects that had been "Christianized." They sold little toy cars and trucks—the same kind you could buy at any discount toy store—but someone stuck a "Jesus loves me" sticker on them, and suddenly they were suitable for sale in a Christian bookstore.

The store carried kazoos, and one day a little boy asked what they were. So Steve demonstrated how to use a kazoo, but cautioned, "This is a Christian kazoo, and it will only play 'Jesus Loves Me, This I Know.'"

The kid stared at him with amazement, took the toy, and ran off to show his mom the amazing Christian kazoo.

Steve is no longer working at that store, which is probably a good thing because his "cynicism-ometer" was starting to peg out in the red zone.

Laughter—good, clean laughter—is good for the soul. It is even good for your health. Ask your doctor; he'll confirm it. I don't think we need to justify laughter—or kazoos—by Christianizing them. Let's get over this guilt thing.

And, yes, I *do* get paid for blathering about nothing. This chapter is a case in point. So *you* just wasted a bunch of hard earned money on *nothing*. Talk about *lousy* stewardship of your resources. I hope you have the decency to feel guilty about it.

Study Guide Question

1. I can even write study guides that say nothing. Do you find this irritating?

 **8**

Sort of Unsolved Mysteries

It is a raging mystery to this very day. One afternoon our church office manager, Robin, opened a large manila envelope that had mysteriously arrived on her desk.

Inside she found an official-looking document that read as follows:

Memorandum

> **TO:** The Ministerial Staff
> **FROM:** The Committee on Appropriate Ministerial Rectitude and Circumspection
> **RE:** Inappropriate Behavior by the Ministerial Staff

It has come to the attention of the Committee on Appropriate Ministerial Rectitude and Circumspection that members of the ministerial staff are driving automobiles with inappropriate colors of paint. The Committee feels compelled to address this crucial issue.

The Committee is deeply concerned, for example, by reports that the church secretary drives a white car. Inasmuch as white is the symbolic color of purity, the Committee is concerned that the use of a white-colored car could represent a haughty, "holier than thou"—or, even worse—"holier than the Committee" mentality. This constitutes a clear and flagrant violation of Saint Paul's directive to "avoid even the appearance of evil" and "esteem others as more impertinent than yourself."

In a related vein, the Committee notes that another member of the ministerial staff drives a blue vehicle. Regrettably, blue is often associated with profane music—such as "the blues"—which is often performed in dark saloons and lounges where pasty-faced loan sharks leer at cocktail waitresses. The Committee does not feel it is either appropriate or circumspect to encourage the flock to frequent these establishments.

The Committee would comment on the remaining colors of ministerial staff automobiles, but modesty prevents us from discussing them. Suffice it to say that some members of the ministerial staff have their minds in the gutter.

Having outlined the biblical basis for our decision, the Committee on Appropriate Ministerial Rectitude and Circumspection hereby directs the ministerial staff—in keeping with the biblical truth that we are "formed from dust, and to dust you shall return"—to drive automobiles that are a dirty brown color. This will also help foster ministerial humility. And for the record, the Committee prefers Fords. They require a lot of faith.

The memo was not attributed to anyone other than the unidentified "Committee on Appropriate Ministerial Rectitude and Circumspection." (Motto: "We Already Know Who We Are, So You Don't Have To.")

More memos appeared in the months to follow. The Committee had an opinion on every facet of church life, from the appropriate color of the choir robes (blue, like heaven) to the appropriate temperature of the water in the baptistery (fifty-eight degrees): "The Committee does not believe in frittering away scarce financial resources heating the baptistery when there are more pressing needs, such as erecting covered parking spaces for members of the Committee. Besides, the Committee has already been baptized."

January dawned with yet another memo slipped through the door of the church office: "The Committee on Appropriate Ministerial Rectitude and Circumspection relishes the dawning of a new year in which the ministerial staff may benefit from our collective wisdom and direction. We trust that the ministerial staff shares our enthusiasm to expose, and then vigorously weed out, the flaws of the ministerial staff. *We* certainly enjoy it."

The anonymous memos were relentless, pounding away at every ministry decision, every expense, *everything*—including the footwear of the high school youth group: "The Committee suggests black wing-tip shoes, inasmuch as this is what the disciples would have worn if they had the opportunity to benefit from the Committee's direction. As always, the Committee is pleased to offer its guidance, and eagerly awaits the opportunity to spy out yet another issue that we can summarily roast with the flame-thrower of vigilance before it grows up into the tender plant of excessive liberty. (The Committee just *loves* these kinds of metaphors.)"

Tragically, these mysterious memos began taking their toll on the staff. Finger pointing abounded. Even worse, all the fingers were pointed at *me*.

One day the pastor for children, Paul, flatly declared that I was involved.

"Do you honestly think that *I* am a member of the Committee?" I replied, aghast.

"No, I think you ARE the Committee," he groused.

The Committee seemed to lose interest after a while, perhaps because their orders were ridiculed and then ignored by the staff. However, the Committee returned with a vengeance when the church began consideration of a building program after it completely maxed out the existing facility and had to begin turning people away.

MEMORANDUM

TO: The Ministerial Staff
FROM: The Committee on Appropriate
Ministerial Rectitude and
Circumspection
RE: The Church Growth Crisis

The Committee on Appropriate Ministerial Rectitude and Circumspection is pleased to inform the Ministerial Staff that we have fashioned a cost-free solution to the distressing problem of church growth (a problem that is making it increasingly difficult for Committee members to sit in their favorite pew).

The Committee, alarmed by the possibility that building new buildings could absorb resources that could otherwise be used to erect covered preferential parking slots for Committee members, has devised a plan to limit this unwanted growth.

The Committee proposes fixing a maximum number of church attendees, and once that limit is reached, the Committee would commence a "weeding-out process" to remove the least desirable members. Thus for every new congregant accepted into our number, the Committee would give the "heave-ho" to the least desirable member. The Committee envisions a specially designed chair attached to an extremely powerful spring, or perhaps even a catapult. While this plan would entail the cost of a moveable "skylight" window, the Committee notes that this modest remodel would cost far less than an entirely new building.

Ever eager to serve, the Committee has volunteered to immediately begin the weeding-out process. While you might expect the Committee to sharply differ over just who, precisely, merits the distinction of the least desirable church member, the Committee is pleased to report a unanimous verdict—Pastor Paul.

The Committee did have trouble coming to a conclusion about where to situate the "heave-ho" seat. Initially, several committee members wished to locate it at the rear of the auditorium so as not to disrupt the service by launching the unfortunate undesirable attendee through the roof. However, after much contemplation, the Committee realized the advantage of placing the special seat right up front. The Committee believes that a very public launching would motivate other service attendees to get their spiritual act together in order to avoid selection for the "heave-ho." Additionally, the spectacle of Pastor Paul hurling into the atmosphere is a sight that, frankly, we would feel selfish for keeping to ourselves. The Committee is magnanimous in this way.

We trust that the ministerial staff (well, at least *most* of the staff) will applaud the Committee's resolution of the disturbing church growth problem. We look forward to a most exciting Sunday morning.

Paul was able to talk the building committee out of this plan. Sadly, he still suspects *me* of setting him up. I think this kind of suspicious, hostile attitude is unbecoming to a member of the ministerial staff.

Looks like it's time for another memo.

Study Guide Questions

1. Don't you agree that people like Pastor Paul should not make reckless accusations when they do not have enough proof to stand up in court?

2. Try telling that to Paul! He almost bit my head off. I think members of the ministerial staff should be more deferential to members of the Committee.

3. I once saw a plaque that read: "For God so loved the world that He did not send a committee." Discuss this with your fellow committee members.

 **9**

Without a Prayer

I think the whole idea of prayer has been hugely over-sold—kind of like time-share vacations. That's why many of us don't spend much time at it. The reality does not match the presentation.

I know a married couple who listened to a great sales pitch from a precious metals enthusiast a few decades ago. They made an enormous financial investment in silver when the price was going through the roof, and then the market crashed. They lost their home over the deal. They felt incredibly stupid, and don't even want to look at silver anymore. It is a reminder of their gullibility. Silver is forever tarnished for them.

I think prayer has likewise been tarnished for a lot of Christian people. It is sold as one thing, but the reality turns out to be something quite different.

So we feel guilty about not praying, because it *is* very clear from the Bible that this is something we are expected to do, but we still don't do it very much. Because for many of us, praying is a painful reminder that prayer is not at all what it has been cracked up to be.

Early in my life I was told things like, "Prayer is a conversation with God" and "You must listen for His voice" and "God will speak if you will but listen."

I was told to look at the example of Moses and Abraham. Why, they had conversations with God all the time! I could be just like them (except for the long robe and legal title to a few thousand sheep).

I took this advice seriously. I tried to have "conversations" with God, but it turned out that I was doing all the talking.

To me, a one-sided conversation is an oxymoron, like "gourmet Cheez Whiz" or "gangster Baptists."

I confessed that prayer didn't seem to be working very well, but I was told if I was not hearing God speak, it was my fault, not His. "He is speaking, you just need to listen better."

It was much later I learned that, in "Christianese," the word *voice* does not mean "voice," *speak* does not mean "speak," *hear* does not mean "hear," and *conversation* does not mean "conversation." This kind of verbal gymnastics reminds me of a legal deposition, where *is* doesn't mean "is" and *alone* means "well, there were other people in the same hemisphere, so no, I can't say I was 'alone.'"

What a gyp! No wonder so many people are burned

out on prayer! Someone has done a "bait and switch" with the English language.

The conversations that Moses and Abraham had with God were, in fact, *real* conversations. They weren't "spiritual impressions" that these guys "sensed" as they "listened with their heart." You don't fall on your face and almost commit a hygienic lapse over a mere "impression."*

With Moses and Abraham, God actually *showed up*— appearing in a burning bush, or in a cloud, or in the form of a being that looked human—and actual audible words were exchanged. That's why we have a record of the conversation.

But there are loads of materials out on the market that still insist our "direction" from God can be as tangible as that of Moses, because, we are told, "There are no second-class citizens with God. He is waiting eagerly to speak with you!"

I disagree.

Moses and Abraham and the prophets were distinctive precisely because God did, in fact, single them out for special one-on-one conversations. The entire Israelite nation was specifically warned by God (through Moses!) that if they *dared* to even *touch* the Holy Mountain while Moses

---

*Unless it is a *really funny* impression, like when Jonathan Winters used to do a version of a little old lady. But that is a not the kind of impression we are talking about here.

was up there talking with God, they would be slain on the spot. I don't know if you can call them "second-class citizens," but you gotta admit there is a bit of a difference between "personal audience with God" and "instant death."

It is true that the New Testament says that all believers can now enter "boldly," and equally, into God's presence via prayer, but nowhere does it say that we are going to have the same kind of "conversations" that marked the prophets.

In fact, when Jesus gave us the model we call "the Lord's Prayer," there is no hint of any reciprocating words back from God. If the model was supposed to be a conversation along the lines of what you have with your spouse, I think He would have said so.

God is not the one who has oversold prayer. Humans are the culprits. In many cases, these have been well-intentioned humans. But I think they have done a lot of damage and burned out a lot of people by making unsubstantiated claims about the nature of prayer.

Prayer is fundamentally *our* communication *to* God. It is a way in which we profess to Him our adoration, confess our sins, take Him up on his offer to listen to our concerns, and even ask things of Him. It is also, indeed, a time when we can be meditative, allow Him to bring to our mind Scripture we have read, or insight to a problem, or sins yet to be confessed. I am not saying that God does not spiritually *relate* to us in prayer. I think He does. But it cannot be equated to a chat with another person.

Prayer is a Christian *discipline*. I think it will always be somewhat of a struggle, precisely because it is an act of faith offered to a God we cannot see or hear or touch. If He were chatting back and forth with us, I would be praying all the time! It would be *fascinating* to turn to God and ask. "Would you mind explaining what a 'leviathan' is? Also, I have always been unclear on the whole 'consider it all joy when you encounter suffering' concept. Would you mind taking it from the top on that one?"

The apostle Paul tells us we will, in fact, one day see God "face to face."*

The implication is that we can also someday have a two-way conversation with Him.

But until then, let us pray.

---

*1 Corinthians 13:12

Study Guide Questions

1. If you disagree, you can pray for me.

2. Yeah, I do think that a lot of folks are taking their own thoughts or desires and presuming that they are getting a message from God.

3. God has spoken, and continues to speak, through the written record we call the Bible. So why are we so reluctant to look there for answers? I think we may prefer the subjectivity of prayer to the objective, and often unwelcome, message of the Bible.

Chapter 10

Out With the Old

I yanked viciously on the lawn mower cord for the zillionth time. The motor spluttered, gasped, and died.

"This is a piece of junk!" I groused. "I'm taking it to the dump and getting a new one."

"When's the last time you checked the spark plug?" Dale asked, looking up from the plant she was watering.

"It isn't the spark plug!" I grumped. "This thing has been around too long! Let's invoke term limits and throw the bum out."

"But when did you change the spark plug?" she repeated.

"Well, let's see," I mused. "Carter had just signed that Panama Canal thing, so . . . late seventies, I think."

It turned out to be the spark plug. It cost me two bucks to get it purring like a kitten, albeit a rather *loud* kitten that spewed exhaust fumes.

I am always either throwing something away, or

attempting to throw something away, or getting caught throwing something away. I have no patience. I am a go, go, go, let's-just-get-it-done kind of guy.

I am continually reminding Dale that as a busy professional I have more money than time. This always results in her falling down on the ground in a laughing heap. But the point remains that it *would* be true if I were rich, so I still have a good argument.

"Do you think a brain surgeon would try to repair his hedge trimmers, or just buy some new ones?" I asked Dale one day as I dangled the trimmers above the trash can.

"Let's make a deal," she offered. "If you become a brain surgeon, you can buy an entirely new hedge. As an added bonus, as a surgeon you'll be able to eliminate the middleman and personally operate on that part of your mind that compels you to throw away perfectly good tools that just need to be oiled."

The frustrating thing about Dale is that she is usually right. She has saved us a small fortune by insisting that I take the time to see if something is truly broken beyond the reasonable possibility of repair. But I still get impatient, and my initial impulse is to hurl stuff into the dumpster.

I didn't get this bad habit from my parents, who survived the aftermath of the Great Depression and tend to fix and save everything that is fixable and savable. I think I have been heavily influenced by my generation, which takes a "disposable" view of the world.

My parents did not grow up with fast food places on every downtown corner. The cars were slower, President Eisenhower had not yet ushered in the Interstate Highway system, and space travel was confined to comic book fantasies. Television was in its infancy. Money was tight. "Entertainment" consisted mostly of visiting with other people—playing games, doing stuff outdoors, or hanging out on the big front porch. It was a completely different world.

Mine is the age of microwaves, cell phones, palm pilots, the Internet, and extraordinarily fast computers that become obsolete about thirty-eight seconds after we plug them in. I think the disposable mentality and dizzying pace of our world has fostered an impatient "throw it out" attitude—an attitude that even spills over into our view of other people.

Spouses are disposable. Children are expendable. People are just like gadgets. If they don't work out like we wanted, we just chuck 'em. Let's go, go, go!

I remember the day a few years ago when my boss and I were invited to visit the Good News Rescue Mission in my hometown. The invitation actually came at a terribly inconvenient time. I had a SCHEDULE to keep, for crying out loud! However, I crammed the appointment in among several other obligations that day.

We walked through the doors of the aging cinder-block building and time somehow ground to a halt. On every floor we found "disposable people." The throwaways of society. Moms and children who had been abandoned by husbands and fathers and suddenly found themselves living in an old car. Grizzled old men who had over the years ingested staggering amounts of alcohol, which was now exacting serious revenge on their livers. Dejected young men who finally hit bottom and were wondering if they could possibly start over—finally free from the jealous clutch of illegal drugs.

That visit led to other visits—sometimes to the Mission, but also to other "recovery homes" in the area. Each visit was a revelation.

I was surrounded by the people I had never found time to even think about, much less get to know—even superficially. They were not part of my white-collar world. But as I listened to their stories—stories of abuse and rejection compounded by tragic choices with terrible ramifications—I saw them in a profoundly new way. They were not throwaways. They were broken people in need of repair.

The mission director, an incredibly kind and compassionate guy named Bill, told me that he sees himself in the men who come in the door on any given day.

"I was heading in the same direction," he confessed. "I hadn't hit bottom; I managed to look pretty good on the outside, but I was heading there."

But Bill fell into the grace of God. He saw the life transformation that was taking place at a rescue mission, and he was hooked. Bill and his sweet wife, Sandra, positively delight in bringing new hope and new life to the people the world has tossed out with the weekly trash.

The Mission is not just a place for down-and-out people to grab a meal and a bed for the night. It is a spiritual repair shop, where love, care, and truth are the tools employed to restart many a gasping, sputtering life.

I was privileged to attend a Good News "graduation" about a year after that initial visit to the Mission. There were quite a few misty eyes in the audience as graduates shared their before-and-after stories.

"I was a hopeless dope addict, and now I am a dopeless hope addict," quipped one graduate.

One man noted with a grin, "A rescue mission is the only operation where you can stumble through the door drunk, and then become the president of the company."

God runs the only fix-it shop where the repaired stuff is actually better than the original.

Study Guide Questions

1. Have you ever had the opportunity to talk with someone who was once on skid row or addicted to drugs
   and then was given a fresh start by the grace of God?

2. If not, then please seek these folks out and listen to
   their story. You'll learn a lot, and it will deepen your
   own faith.

3. If you are one of those restored people, please tell us
   about it. I'd love to get a letter from you.

4. If you are a brain surgeon, at least you have a huge
   income tax bill. So there. Not that I am deeply jealous
   of your income or the fact that YOU don't have to
   trim your own hedges.

Section 3

Various and Sundry mutterings

Chapter 11

Cry "Uncle!"

Uncle Ray came to our home on a seasonal basis, kind of like the swallows returning year after year to San Juan Cappuccino or wherever it is they return to. He would appear for a season, move into a spare bedroom, make us laugh, and then move on after a couple of months.

He was a bit of a mystery to me, but I loved him a lot. He always seemed to have money, but he only worked when he wanted to. He disappeared into his room and listened for hours at a time to really sad songs by Johnny Cash—songs about prison and grief. He soaked up music like a paper towel soaks up spilled coffee. It colored him through and through. When there was nothing left to soak up, he would turn off the music and go bowling. I think he would have lived at the bowling alley if they would have put up a cot there and let him fill the jukebox with sad Johnny Cash songs.

One afternoon he told me that he "bowled 300" that day.

That sounded like an awful lot of games for one afternoon, and I didn't believe him, even though I was just a gullible five-year-old kid.

I never knew when to believe Uncle Ray. It wasn't like he lied, it's just that he was always pulling my leg about something and then laughing about it. He had a laugh like Barney Rubble in the Flintstones cartoon. He was the funnest uncle you could have. He would bowl with me, and I would win. I didn't know if he was letting me win. I didn't care. Ray had time for us kids even when other adults were too busy because they had to work. Ray had more free time than any adult I knew.

"How are you doing, little brother?" my dad would ask when Ray came back to our house again after vanishing for nine or ten months.

"Finer than frog's hair," Ray would reply with a big grin and a chuckle.

He had only a few suitcases. Ray traveled light. Ray was a drifter, just like the people in the sad songs.

Mom and Dad would whisper about Ray sometimes, but stop when I walked into the room. Even at a very young age, I knew that something was up with Ray, but I had no idea what it was. It was clear that my parents loved Ray, but they seemed to, well, *watch* him a lot. Sometimes

I would hear my dad's voice get loud in the other room when he was with Ray.

"You're going through your money pretty fast there, aren't you Ray?"

"Robert, don't get yourself all worked up," Ray would reply.

Telling my dad not to get worked up did *nothing* if not get him worked up. But Ray said it all the time. I think he actually enjoyed getting my dad worked up, because he would do something to drive Dad crazy and then laugh about it.

Ray could get away with saying stuff that no one else could get away with.

He was a short man. He was so short that he didn't seem like a grown-up. Maybe that was one of the reasons he seemed more like one of us kids than an adult.

One day we were having a big family get-together with a lot of my cousins, and I was chasing one of them through the house because he did something to me, and I grabbed at him but missed him and I shouted, "You reee-tard!" as he dodged my grasp.

My dad whirled around and walked over to me and I knew that this must be a *bad* word like another bad word I said one day, which was apparently so bad that it literally required a bar of soap to get the letters out of my mouth.

Dad stared at me for a moment, and then said, "Never call anyone that word again."

"OK," I said.

"Do you know what that word means?" Dad asked.

"Not exactly," I said. "I think it means something like 'dummy.'"

Dad paused.

"Did you know that your Uncle Ray is retarded?" he asked.

"NO HE ISN'T!" I retorted.

I was not a kid who usually risked talking back to my dad, but I was flushed with outrage that he was calling my Uncle Ray retarded.

"I am not calling Ray a name, son," Dad explained. "A mentally retarded person is not a dumb person. Some mentally retarded people are born with something called 'Down syndrome' that makes them different from you and me. They are slow. They can't learn the same way you and I do. It is like they are always children and they never grow up, even though they get older. That's why Ray lives with us part of the year. He needs someone to take care of him. When your grandmother was dying, she called all of her children into the room and asked us to always take care of Ray. That's why Ray moves from home to home every few months. It gives each of us a chance to have Ray be part of our family, just like my mother asked us to do."

I let this soak in for a minute.

"What grade would Uncle Ray be in?"

"About third grade," Dad replied.

"He sounds a lot smarter than that. He uses big words," I observed.

"Ray prides himself on his use of language," Dad agreed. "But he can barely write. So the third grade thing is not a hard and fast rule. It just gives us an idea of his limitations. Ray can do things like dress himself and make a sandwich, but he can never drive or cook. He can never live alone."

Ray was never an embarrassment to us. To the contrary, he was a huge hit with all of our friends. He was so incredibly friendly and so outrageously funny.

As Dad noted, Ray was extremely precise when it came to the use of the English language.

EXAMPLE: Ray is sitting in the backseat of the car as my dad is preparing to back out of the driveway onto a busy street.

DAD: "Ray, I can't see the traffic. Look both ways for me and tell me if there are any cars coming."

RAY: (Looking both ways) "Nope."

Dad starts backing out, only to have a horn blare at him as a vehicle roars past.

DAD: "Ramon! I thought you said there were no cars coming!"

RAY: "That was not a car. It was a truck."

One hot summer day I was walking home from the store with Ray when he clutched his chest, winced, and said, "Daver, I need to sit down for a minute."

Both of us were operating at third grade level, so neither of us understood he was having a heart attack. I can't quite remember what happened next. I know a concerned motorist stopped and asked if we needed help. Ray said, "No." I think the man got help anyway.

Ray survived, but the doctors put him on a special diet and gave him pills. He seemed to recover OK. But he didn't like the diet.

"Ray, have you been into the chocolate syrup?" my mom asked one day.

"What makes you ask that?" Ray replied, bewildered at Mom's apparent ability to peer through walls.

"Oh, just the big ring of chocolate around your mouth, and chocolate syrup all over the counter."

Ray was kind of fanatical about cleaning his glasses. He would disappear into the bathroom for thirty or forty minutes at a time and swipe the lenses with a tissue, then put the glasses on, take them off, put them on again, and take them off. Sometimes I would hammer on the door and shout, "They're clean enough! I need to go!"

One day my dad needed to use the bathroom, and he called to Ray to clean his glasses later, and Ray did not reply.

"Ray!" Dad said a bit louder, shaking the doorknob.

No answer.

No sound.

"RAY!" Dad shouted, banging on the door.

Silence.

Then Dad completely lost it. I thought he was madder than I had ever seen him, but looking back on it later I realized it was raw panic.

"Get my tools!" Dad yelled.

We were all staring at the door as Dad feverishly dismantled the doorknob.

"RAMON!"

No reply.

Time ground to a crawl, like when a movie drops into slow motion to draw out the agony of a rescue scene.

Dad fairly ripped the door off the hinges.

And there we found Ray.

He was standing in front of the mirror, methodically cleaning his glasses—the very picture of health.

"RAMON!!!" my dad yelled. "What in the world are you trying to do to us?!!?"

Ray swiped his lens one last time lest he missed a dirt molecule, put his glasses back on, and replied, "Robert, don't get yourself all worked up."

If there were a National Teeth-Gritting & Jugular-Bulging Competition, Dad would have won it hands down.

Ray just laughed his Barney Rubble laugh.

Dad took several aspirin.

One day we were sitting in church, and throughout the entire sermon about the Good Shepherd, Ray, as usual, was fidgeting with his watch, his glasses, his wallet, his coins, and just about any other fidget-worthy item.

Later that day Mom said, "Bob, he's not paying any attention and he's distracting everyone else."

Dad nodded slowly.

"Maybe we should stop taking him if it is just a waste of time," Dad said.

Mom agreed.

Dad turned to Ray.

"Ray, do you know what a shepherd is?"

Ray gave a big sigh, rolled his eyes, and replied, "Anybody knows that. If one of the little baa-baas gets lost, the shepherd goes way out into the moondocks and searches until he finds it, and then he will pick it up and put it on his shoulders and bring it back home."

Mom and Dad's eyes filled with tears.

"And I know *all about* the King of heaven," Ray added.

That ended any discussion of not taking him to church.

Ray continued to live with Mom and Dad, on his rotating schedule, long after all five of the Meurer kids moved out on our own. Moving eventually got to be too much change for him, so he just settled in for the long haul. In a sense, Mom and Dad never had an empty nest. There was always a third grader at home.

Ray was sixty-three when the Good Shepherd put him on His shoulders and brought the little baa-baa home.

Cry "Uncle!"

Whenever I hear some medical "ethicist" say it is perfectly OK, perhaps even morally necessary, to "terminate" people the "ethicist" feels will not have a sufficient "quality of life," I remember my uncle Ray.

And I get all worked up.

I hope you will too.

Study Guide Questions

1. There is a professor named Dr. Peter Singer who at the date of this writing is chairman of Bioethics at Princeton University's Center for Human Values. He has written that parents who find themselves with what he terms a "defective" infant should be able to legally kill the baby within the first month after birth. Read on:

2. "The only difference between killing a normal infant and a defective one is the attitude of the parents" (*Practical Ethics*, by Dr. Peter Singer, 1993).

   "Therefore, if killing the hemophiliac infant has no adverse effects on the others, it would, according to the total view [of utilitarianism] be right to kill him. The main point is clear: killing a disabled child is not morally equivalent to killing a person. Very often it is not wrong at all" (from the same book).

3. Do you think it is OK for Christian people to describe Dr. Singer as a "frighteningly dangerous wacko who sounds remarkably like a Nazi?" I do.

4. Folks, we need to speak up about these very dangerous cultural trends. What was *unthinkable* in our nation mere decades ago is becoming mainstream—and innocent lives are hanging in the balance. We need to hear the reasoned, passionate voice of the church.

5. Please make sure you vote in each election. The men and women we elect wield huge influence about the protections afforded or stripped from the powerless and the innocent.

6. Several years ago I was stunned when a very prominent Christian businessman casually mentioned to me that he was actively supporting—and even giving money to—a congressional candidate who was just *terrible* on key social issues. This awful candidate, however, did support a federal program that directly benefited the businessman. The businessman apparently saw my jaw hit the floor, because he shrugged and said, "When it comes to politics, you have to vote your wallet." *Says who?* How about doing the *right* thing, even if it hurts your narrow self-interest?

Chapter 12

Soul Music

For the past several decades, one question has troubled churches more than just about any other. And that vexing question is: "Why isn't the Holy Land actually blue like it shows on our Bible maps?"

This question demonstrates that theological awareness is in the tank these days, because scholarly research has proven that the Holy Land is actually orange like it shows on the globe.

But a second question has also registered pretty high on the church vexation scale, and that question is: "What kind of music does God like?"

Most of us secretly believe that He likes the kind of music we like. But we have nothing to base that on, because the Bible is not at all clear on this issue. Even if we agree on a set of words, we can put those words to radically different styles and tempos of music, with wildly differing instruments.

I recently heard a high school youth group kid playing "I Have Decided to Follow Jesus" on his car stereo in the church parking lot. But the song could just as easily have been titled "I Have Decided to Deafen Jesus," because there was so much bass blasting from the speakers that the car windows were literally bulging in and out, and the shock waves were knocking small birds off branches at fifty yards away.

What did God think of that?

I was raised in a religious tradition that was very formal, very traditional, and very reserved. When it came to God, there was only one kind of music and that was *organ* music. And we are not talking about one of those dinky little keyboard things that sort of looks like an organ but really isn't. We are talking about a real, solid oak organ that was bigger than a Volvo station wagon and weighed twice as much. If you would have slapped four tires on that organ and put it on the freeway, it could have passed for a Winnebago. So we are talking a *serious* organ.

People at my church were quiet. We filed in very placidly and somberly and reverently, and eased into our hard, unpadded oak pews where we learned the meaning of *suffering* for our faith.

We weren't like the noisy, hugging, back-slapping evangelicals with their padded seats and pianos and . . . drums.

Drums? In church?

Do you think the apostles had drums in *their* gatherings?

I think not!

No, the apostles had enormous Wurlitzer organs with three levels of keys, just like my church had.

Drums?

As far as we were concerned, the next step down that slippery slope might be a fog machine and a big disco ball with all those little mirrors.

Well, *we* were certainly not going to go down that road. *We* knew what kind of music God liked, and He liked the organ, and the only tragedy is that He never quite got around to mentioning it to Saint Paul or it would be in the Bible and we wouldn't have to keep arguing about it.

It took a long time for me to get used to being a Protestant. I'm getting there, but it still isn't easy. Being from a formal, liturgical background, there are some things that I am still just not used to—like people raising their hands during worship services. I know that it is biblical, and that the psalmist says, "I will lift up my hands unto Thy name." But it is not what I grew up with, so it is way out of my comfort zone.

I once did a poll of our congregation, which is composed of people from all kinds of church backgrounds.

"How many of you were raised in a more formal church background?"

About a third of the hands went up.

"How many of you are uncomfortable with raising your hands in church?"

About half the hands went up.

"Well, now what do we do?" I asked. "If we put up one more hand, we are basically just like the radicals that do all that hugging."

I think some of them are still recovering from the experience. I know I am.

There is a great scene in *The Muppet Movie*, where Kermit the Frog and Fozzie the Bear enter an old abandoned church building where a Muppet band is playing some pretty loud jazzy music. There are electric guitars, drums, a keyboard, and a saxophone.

Fozzie turns to Kermit and says, "They don't look like Presbyterians to me!"

That is an interesting statement, and it raises a logical series of questions. First, what *should* a Presbyterian look like? Is there a standard height, weight, clothing style, toothpaste brand, or musical taste for Presbyterians?

When the Muppet said, "They don't look like Presbyterians to me," what he was really saying is that "Christians should look and sound a certain way."

Well, what *should* a Christian look and sound like?

One day I came into church and saw, seated in the front row, a big, burly biker-looking dude dressed in a black leather coat. He had a wild beard and frazzled gray hair. I thought to myself, *Well, I'm glad this large biker person has come to church today. I hope he learns something. I just hope he doesn't make a scene.*

Well, he did make a scene. He got up and quoted several chapters of the gospel of John verbatim from memory, and then he came back that night and quoted the entire book of Revelation.

He didn't look like a Presbyterian to me!

But again, what should a Christian look like? What should a Christian sound like? What kind of music should a Christian make?

When I was a kid, I assumed that God liked organ music simply because it is what I grew up listening to during religious services. I think many of us make these kinds of huge illogical leaps. Our preferences and habits are projected on to God.

So what kind of music does God like?

Is it the organ? The harp? The guitar? How about an electric guitar? Or how about that weird, twanging, strange music they play in the Middle East? To me, it sounds like a bunch of over-wound clock springs being broken. And it is probably pretty much what Jesus grew up listening to. And He probably *liked* it.

And what about the instruments they play in China or India? Those sounds just aren't sounds I like.

But what does God think about it?

Can He like sounds that are very different from my preconceived notions about music that is Christian?

Hmmmm . . .

Perhaps God likes all music that is offered up to Him by people who love Him and who seek to honor Him. That definition has enough room for every child of God, of any nation, age, group, or culture.

Technically, that definition could include a big disco ball and a fog machine, but let's not push it, young people.

I will end this discussion where the Psalms—God's music book—ends. This is the final psalm:

Praise the Lord.
Praise God in his sanctuary;
    praise him in his mighty heavens.
Praise him for his acts of power;
    praise him for His surpassing greatness.
Praise him with the sounding of the trumpet,
    praise him with the harp and lyre,
praise him with tambourine and **dancing**,
    [do NOT get me started on THAT]
    praise him with the strings and flute,
praise him with the clash of cymbals,
    praise him with resounding cymbals.
Let everything that has breath praise the Lord.
Praise the Lord.

—Psalm 150

Study Guide Questions

1. Nevertheless, old hymns are still the best. Just deal with it.

2. The author maintains that while technically accurate, the song performed by a group called The Newsboys, wherein the singers inform us that breakfast is not served in hell, does not hold a candle to ANYTHING ever penned by Isaac Watts, even though the author has to agree the song kind of grows on you after a while.

3. The author had no choice but to learn this song after the author's boys played it 6,000 times in a row when the CD was originally released.

4. Don't you agree that the author, like all parents of teen boys, puts up with a *lot?*

5. Try convincing his kids. They think they are practically martyrs.

College Daze

I was sitting in a college class discussing other cultures, when I inadvertently used a naughty word that brought the entire class to a halt.

The word was *uncivilized*.

Specifically, I had referred to the cultural custom, formerly practiced in India, of burning alive the living widow of a deceased male.

"It was uncivilized, and the British were right to put an end to it," I said.

All heck broke loose.

"That is ethnocentric!"

"That presumes one people has the right to impose its own morality on another people!"

"The term 'uncivilized' is a value judgment!"

I then did another bad thing. I stuck to my position.

"I believe in value judgments. World War II was, in large part, a huge value judgment. The Nazis and the

Fascists had a morally inferior position that allowed un-provoked aggression and the wholesale slaughter of entire groups of people. The United States and the Allied armies were right to stop them by force."

Oodles more heck broke loose.

"So are you saying that all Americans were morally superior to all Germans or Italians?" huffed one student.

"No, but I am saying that the position of America was morally superior to what Hitler stood for."

"I disagree with Hitler's position, but I don't think I would use the term 'morally superior,'" chimed in another student. "I would be comfortable saying that I personally disagreed with him, but I don't see how we can say we were 'morally right' and he was 'morally wrong' because morality is a culturally determined thing. It isn't as though there is a single, objective standard that exists out there."

I am not making this stuff up. This exchange actually took place. On college campuses today, it is entirely possible to find lots of students who are unwilling to say that Adolph Hitler was morally wrong by any universal standard. They'll be quick to say they disagree with him, that they are repulsed by him, that they would have resisted him—but they can't say he was "wrong" by any objective, transcendent moral law because they do not believe there is an objective, transcendent moral law. All that exists is individual preference.

"Let's do a role play," I suggested. "Let's pretend that I

am a guy named Heinrich Himmler and you are all Jews. I have a gun, and you do not. We are in Germany in 1942. It is the official position of the German government that Jews are an inferior race who must be eliminated. If morality is determined by the culture, then I would be on morally defensible ground to put a bullet into your brain. Convince me not to shoot, or I will open fire on you one by one."

There was a stunned silence. Finally, one student spoke up.

"I would try to persuade him that Jews are not inferior."

"I'm unconvinced," I replied.

BLAM!

One down, twenty to go.

"I would say that I personally disagree with taking an innocent life," ventured another.

"Your disagreement has been noted," I replied.

BLAM!

I continued to pick them off, one by one, because not one student could articulate any reason other than some form of the statement, "I disagree with you."

Finally, an exasperated student snapped, "I don't think it is fair for you to throw these kinds of hypothetical situations at us."

"It isn't hypothetical," I retorted. "There really was a guy named Himmler, and he worked under Hitler, and eliminating Jews was in his job description. And you can't even tell the guy that what he is doing is wrong, because you don't believe in any objective standard of right and wrong. All you have are preferences. But he has his own preferences. And he prefers to have you dead."

BLAM!

"Do you realize the enormity of what you believe?" I asked. "You are saying that throwing people in an oven or not throwing them in an oven are nothing more than issues of personal preference. It is precisely that kind of thinking that makes genocide possible. Someone please give Himmler a reason not to pull the trigger again. Even if he ignores you, give him something better than 'I disagree with your preference.' "

I finally ended up facing a young woman who looked me in the eye and said, "God will judge you for every innocent life you take."

That was one of the few rational thoughts uttered that day.

The period ended and the class was dismissed.

As I made my way toward my next class, a student ran up to me. It was the guy who complained that my "hypothetical" situation was unfair.

"I really do believe that Hitler was wrong," he said, his brow furrowed in dismay.

"Was he wrong by any universally binding standard?

Or do you just mean you personally don't like what he did?"

The poor guy was in agony. Every commonsense impulse in him told him to agree that Hitler was a moral atrocity. His own conscience was almost audibly screaming at him to agree that throwing babies into an oven is a horrific moral outrage that is a universal WRONG! But years of university nonsense had persuaded him that only a cretin believed that some things are always right and some things are always wrong. In the end, all he could do was tell me that, *personally*, he really, really, really disagreed with Hitler.

He kept walking with me.

Finally, I turned to him and said, "You *know* deep down that genocide is *wrong*. You *know* it because in your heart you are better than your creed."

We parted company on that note.

Study Guide Questions

1. Scary, isn't it?

2. Ideas have consequences.

3. When people believe that there is no God, or believe in a god of their own making, then universally binding standards of right and wrong are toast, and everyone is at risk.

4. Have you recently talked to some teens—perhaps even your own—about what they believe about the universe? About truth, and right and wrong? I'd suggest it.

Chapter 14

Fishing Diary

DAY 1

The key to successful fishing is to be named Walt.

I learned this today when my friend Dan and I brought to Oregon's Umpqua River every conceivable item of fishing gear produced by Western civilization in the past several centuries—including neoprene waders, an array of lures more expensive than the crown jewels of France, and even fashionable T-shirts with fishing logos—but the only guy who caught a fish was Walt.

He was using some cheap plastic round thing that only a complete moron of a fish would mistake for a salmon egg, but steelhead fled from our $5.95 Mepps lures like they were toxic waste and lunged instead at Walt's glob of plastic as though it were the last morsel of food on the planet. If the average steelhead is stupid enough to fall for Walt's inexpensive treachery, then everything *Field &*

Stream has ever published is a filthy lie. The editors just realize that the day they run a story titled "Only Guys Named Walt Will Catch a Fish" is the day they sell their last magazine. But now their little secret is out.

Walt insists that the real key to fishing is abandoning all personal hygiene for the duration of the trip. He says filth "covers up" the human scent. We believe he is just trying to keep us from scampering down to the courthouse to have our names legally changed to "Walt."

DAY 2

Today I learned that plunging into the freezing Umpqua River is something you probably want to avoid, especially when you have your outlandishly expensive Nikon camera slung around your neck. Although I demonstrated that this is a bad idea, Dan insisted on trying it himself. Bear in mind that we are both *paying* for this experience. Walt, on the other hand, escaped unscathed. The disturbing "Walt Trend" thus continues.

Dan and I are increasingly suspicious.

We made Walt sleep near an open window tonight.

DAY 3

Another member of our fishing excursion, Lyle, has landed a salmon the approximate weight and dimensions of Winston Churchill. He was not using Walt's cheap plastic egg, and he also regularly brushes his teeth. And, tellingly, he was not sporting a fake "Hi! My name is Walt" name badge like Dan and I were.

While this breaks the disturbing Walt Trend, it also blows my initial theory regarding why I have caught nothing. Perhaps my fishing logo T-shirts are insufficiently attractive to our prey. Tomorrow I shall boldly switch to a forest green sweatshirt emblazoned with the words "Catch and Release." This may convince them that I mean no harm. In reality, I have already purchased a substantial quantity of mesquite briquettes and cleaned the ashes from my Weber.

Inasmuch as Lyle is a minister, I have taken the opportunity to probe deep theological questions, such as: "Since Jesus called His followers to become 'fishers of men,' wouldn't it be considered moral laxity for a minister to leave that high calling and become a mere fisher of fish?"

He said I can't have his salmon, and that if he catches me near his ice chest again he will phone the authorities. Clearly, I have touched a raw nerve and he is wracked with guilt.

Meanwhile, Walt is violating federal clean air standards each time he raises his arm to cast.

DAY 4

Dan and I groused to the lady at the tackle shop about our bad luck. She suggested that we try a "Dupont Spinner" which, she chuckled, is a euphemism for dynamite.

We asked what aisle it was in, and she grew serious and said she was just joking and then made disparaging comments about our sportsmanship. What a cruel hoax.

Dan is growing particularly edgy and has purchased sixteen additional fashionable T-shirts, which he changes every few minutes. Lyle is basking in the glow of success, and Walt is wearing a halo of flies. We make him fish WAY downwind from us.

Dan and I must pack our bags and go home tomorrow to face the ridicule of defeat. At least it isn't just me getting skunked.

TAIL END OF DAY 4

Dan has landed a steelhead the size of an apartment complex.

He was not wearing a fishing logo T-shirt at the time. And he was using a four-pound test line, which is akin to dragging a submarine to shore with dental floss.

The key to successful fishing is to not be named Dave.

Maybe I'll go try that "fisher of men" thing that Lyle keeps talking about. It doesn't require special T-shirts, it is less smelly, and if you succeed you don't even have to gut anything.

Study Guide Questions

1. Would you agree that Walt's disgusting and revolting personal habits while fishing are, for lack of a better term, "disgusting and revolting"? Me too.

2. But let's suppose he could actually *prove* you would catch more fish if you reeked like a hog rendering plant in the middle of July. Would you imitate him?

3. You fishing fanatics are sick.

Chapter 15

Under the influence

I kept my drinking excesses a secret until the day an empty container, stashed hurriedly under the seat of my car, rolled on to the floorboard when I had to step hard on the brakes at a stoplight. It was picked up by my son Brad, then fourteen years old.

"And just what would *this* be?" he asked, wide-eyed, fingering the container.

I was caught. Nailed.

My mind raced back to that hot summer day that I pulled into the parking lot and, on impulse, grabbed a quick one for the road. I had downed it before I reached the office. My colleague didn't suspect a thing. But I had neglected to toss the container.

"I can explain," I stammered.

"Try," he replied.

"It was a really hot day."

"There's always water," he retorted. "After all the

lectures, I can't *believe* this! Wait until I tell Mom and Mark!"

We drove home in tense silence.

I pulled into the driveway and Brad leapt from the car and bounded up the steps to the front door.

"Mark!" Brad called to his brother. "Look what Dad's been doing behind our backs!"

Mark stared at the empty container and yelped, "You've been sucking down Baskin Robbins Mocha Blasts behind our backs? Those things cost three bucks each!"

"I had a coupon," I said weakly.

"How many have you had?" Brad demanded.

"Two or three," I replied. "Ten at the max."

"And this is the same dad who lectures us about being *frugal?*" Brad scoffed. "Is this the same Mr. Hey-Kids-Let's-Make-Our-Own-Milkshakes-at-Home-and-Save-Money?"

They forced me back into the car and made me shell out my own money for two large Cappuccino Blasts with whipped cream and cinnamon.

Lessons learned:

1. All secrets will be revealed.
2. So don't even try to get away with anything.
3. But if you are going to have a secret drinking problem, just make sure it is something that you wouldn't terribly mind your kids drinking, because it is highly likely that they will.

Study Guide Questions

1. Do you think God sometimes actually orchestrates things so that something you are trying to hide gets exposed? I do.

2. But it is for our own good.

3. Is there any secret you would like to share with your group and thus beat God to the punch?

4. Do your kids watch you like a hawk for the slightest sign of inconsistency? (Hint: The answer is YES.)

Section 4

"Other"

Chapter 16

Flammable Household Appliances (and Other Combustible Close Calls)

Twenty-five years ago a guy named Jerry taught me that the secret to really great barbecued food is simply this: *Never clean the grill.*

"Honest," he said as he observed my wrinkled brow. "The flavor builds up on the metal, and as a bonus you get to avoid the messy job of getting all that grease off the grill."

You'll never read this helpful tip in *Better Homes & Gardens* magazine. But I have been following Jerry's advice for more than two decades now, and I can personally attest to the fact that not cleaning the grill takes a *lot* less time than cleaning the grill. However, my grill has developed a nasty habit of erupting into flames moments after I ignite the propane.*

On one occasion, my neighbors called the fire department to report that a flaming meteorite had apparently crashed into the Meurer's backyard—smack into a pile of pork ribs.

Many forest fires emit less smoke than my barbecue grill. Hostile researchers have begun to blame me for global warming.

"Why don't you just clean it sometime?!!" Dale shouted one day above the roar of the flames as I sprayed water on the bellowing conflagration.

"You lose the flavor!" I called back to her through the smoke.

Confession time: for many years now, I have suspected that Jerry was wrong. Actually, to be perfectly honest, I am *certain* he was wrong. I think he was just looking for a minimally plausible reason to get out of cleaning a sooty, greasy grill. But because he gave me a reasonably decent excuse to avoid a task I'd prefer to avoid anyway, I have been clutching to his words like barnacles seize to the bottom of a boat.

Isn't it amazing how we will kid ourselves, and even outright lie to ourselves, to have our own way?

Sometimes it starts out as wishful thinking—"Hey, it *could* be true"—but even when we suspect that the facts

---

*Oddly, Jerry always seemed to have this problem as well.

are otherwise, we often continue to believe what we want to believe. And we don't just do this about fairly inconsequential issues like scrubbing a grill. Against a mountain of evidence to the contrary, we often hold on to all kinds of myths, because the myths frequently require less from us than the truth.

I recently heard a caller on a radio talk show who was hopping mad when she discovered that her son had been smoking pot with a friend for months in the friend's house.

"Where were the friend's parents?" asked the talk show host.

"Upstairs," replied the unamused mom. "They said they had no idea."

"They didn't *want* to know," replied the host.

And that is probably the case. For crying out loud, even Helen Keller would have at least *smelled* the stuff wafting up the stairs.

Parents lie to themselves about their kids because the truth is much more burdensome to deal with. Who needs the hassle of reality when denial is as close as the TV remote control or a cold beer in the fridge?

Wives will lie to themselves about their alcoholic husbands, and husbands will do the same about their wives' excessive use of diet pills. Church people will lie to themselves about the multiple signs that their pastor is unfaithful to his wife. We'll even lie to ourselves about our favorite president, because we want the myth of leadership if we can't have the real thing.

Some of us have even been known to lie to ourselves about physics.

A few years ago, after procrastinating for weeks, I finally reached the last valid day of my burn permit for leaves and branches and assorted garden debris. I was raking and piling everything into a huge mound when I noticed ominous clouds moving in. It was looking suspiciously like rain. I was piling on the last few branches when a drop of water hit my nose.

The race was on.

I dashed to the garage to grab the bottle of charcoal lighter fluid and found it was virtually empty. DRAT!

I looked wildly around as the telltale tapping of rain sounded on the roof of the garage. The only flammable substance I could find was gasoline.

I grabbed the gas can and matches and ran toward the burn pile, but even as I ran I had a distinct recollection of my sixth grade science teacher telling us that gas fumes are heavier than air and they hug the ground as you fill up your car and that is why if someone tosses a cigarette down at a gas station the entire place could blow up.

"Fortunately, I don't smoke," I said to myself.

Plus, I would only use a little.

The rain increased.

Well, maybe just a quart.

Flammable Household Appliances

I reasoned that I could dump the gasoline on the pile really fast, then stand waaaaay back before the fumes had time to spread out. It couldn't be all that risky, and I needed to beat the rain before it really picked up or I would be stuck with the unsightly pile of debris until the next burn season.

So I doused the pile with gas, then stood back about eight feet and flicked a match.

If you have ever seen one of those old army films they made back in the 1950s when they still did above-ground nuclear bomb detonations, you'll have a rough idea of what happened next, only with less radioactivity.

The flames roared outward with a huge "FOOOMP," hugging the ground and surrounding me in vivid orange heat. The hair on my arms curled up and disappeared. Before I could even take a step back, the air rushed back into the pile and sucked burning leaves into the rising column of flames.

Quickly recovering my wits, I managed to stand there and shriek, "GAAAAAAAAAHHHHH!!!!!"

Dale took the matches away from me for an entire year.

Petty retaliation is so unbecoming to women. As if the loss of my eyebrows wasn't punishment enough. For weeks concerned strangers in store aisles looked at me with the same pity they showed to chemotherapy patients.

The really terrible thing about this incident was that

deep down I knew it was inherently dangerous. Assuring yourself, "Oh, it'll be OK," does not quite rise to the level of peer-reviewed science.

Reality is not dictated by what we wish were true.

Jesus once said, "You shall know the truth, and the truth will set you free." Fundamentally He was speaking about spiritual truth and specifically about the freedom that comes from knowing Him for who He really is. But I think His words have a broader application to all aspects of our life.

Quite simply, we need to look the truth in the face and believe it, no matter how unwelcome it may be. Jesus never said the truth would be easy, only liberating. Truth is often difficult, awkward, inconvenient, and demanding. But it is still the truth.

Any counselor or psychiatrist worth his degree will tell you that much mental illness, self-destructive behavior, and even uncontrolled flames stem from people trying to avoid the truth.

So let us embrace the truth, whatever the cost.

For some of us, that resolution will mean cleaning the barbecue grill for the first time since our national bicentennial. It could also mean a painful conversation with a loved one. It could mean a brutally honest confession to God. But in every case, it ultimately means freedom.

Study Guide Questions

1. Yes, my eyebrows have grown back.

2. Have you ever done something that stupid with flames? Discuss in your small group and invite your children to listen.

3. I recently read a newspaper account about a guy who used gasoline in an attempt to "restart" the embers in his wood stove. I think the fire department was able to salvage at least part of his home. On the downside, I believe his wife also took away his match privileges. What is it about women that makes them so uptight about these little learning episodes?

4. Do you ever find yourself deliberately avoiding any unpleasant truths?

Chapter 17

We, the Genders . . .

"Dad, can you test me on the Declaration of Independence? We have to memorize part of it," Brad said.

"Sure," I replied, delighted that his class was becoming grounded in our founding documents.

"First, I'm going to read it out loud, then I'll try to do it from memory," he said.

"Go for it," I replied.

"We hold these Truths to be self-evident, that all people are created equal—"

"Try again," I interrupted. "You made a little mistake."

Brad stared at the paper in his hands, shrugged, and took another stab at it.

"We hold these Truths to be self-evident, that all people are created equal—"

"Brad, focus on the *words*," I chided. "It says, 'all *men* are created equal.' "

"No, it doesn't," he retorted, handing me the paper the teacher had passed out.

I stared dumbfounded at the cursive script. Thomas Jefferson's immortal words had been *edited* to make them gender neutral.

I felt my blood pressure rising.

"Brad, why don't you go outside and play while Dad pops a few heart pills and calls an ambulance?"

Later I explained to Brad that the Declaration says what it says, despite who it may offend. Ditto the Lord's Prayer, which some liberal churches have dared to alter so that it reads, "Our Creator, which art in heaven." Some of the wackier groups will no doubt go a step further and edit the passage to read, "Our Oppressive Male Deity, whom we don't believe in anyway."

There is something very scary about altering historical documents in order to make them conform to modern-day ideologies.

If this keeps up, you may open a church history volume someday and read about the famous hymn writer who penned "Onward Christian pacifists, marching as to the nuclear disarmament rally."*

If my son's teacher had wanted to explain that there have been many changes since the days of the founding fathers, she could easily have done so. In fact, it would

*And we'll be singing from our *"personal"* instead of our "hymnal." And we won't dare say "*amen*."

128

have been a great opportunity to explain that our Constitution contains a mechanism by which it can be amended, and to point out how that process was utilized to grant women the right to vote, to lower voting age to eighteen, and to amend an offensive section that counted non-whites as partial people.

But misinforming students in order to make history "inclusive" is a sheer outrage. It is lying. It makes a mockery of the very word "educate." It is likewise outrageous to tinker with the Bible.

Frankly, there are lots of things in the Scriptures that jar my sensibilities—such as divine judgments that wiped out thousands of men, women, and children. I have a very hard time understanding some of the stuff I read. But I don't feel the freedom to pull out the scissors and leave the offending passages on the cutting room floor. And I *certainly* can't imagine substituting, "And then the Lord thundered in his wrath, 'You guys knock that off or there will be NO ice cream after the golden calf ribbon-cutting and orgy.'"

Let's go back to the example of the Lord's Prayer for a minute. It may not seem like that big of a deal to change one biblical term, "Father," for another biblical term, "Creator," but the implications are huge. While the Bible refers to God as the Creator, Sustainer, Savior, Lord—and all kinds of other titles—these are not equal terms that you can just pluck out as though you are using a thesaurus.

Those terms have different meanings in order to emphasize a specific attribute of God.

If Jesus had wanted us to pray, "Our Creator," or "Our Redeemer," or "Our Gender Non-Specific Almighty Individual in heaven," He could have and would have said so. But He deliberately selected the word *Father*.

None of us has the right to change the record of what He said. History is history. And while none of us will ever stand before Thomas Jefferson to give an account for messing with his words, we will stand before a God who has emphatically stated that His Word will "endure forever." So let's not get cheeky with God.

In a related vein, whether you like it or not, the English language does not contain a gender-neutral term to refer to an individual. See what I mean in the following sentence.

"If anyone touches Mom's last Snapple raspberry tea, he is going to get whacked with a spatula!"

The term "he" correctly covers both genders. In that sentence there is no substitute for the word *he* unless you are willing to resort to bad grammar.

EXAMPLE: "If anyone touches Mom's last Snapple raspberry tea, them is going to get whacked with a spatula!"

See what I mean?

Some people cheat and just make the sentence plural.

"If anyone touches Mom's last Snapple raspberry tea,

they are going to get whacked with a spatula!"

But that turns "anyone," which is singular, into "they," which is plural. You may be able to get away with referring to an individual in the plural if the person in question is tremendously overweight or has multiple personalities, but you may get slugged.

Some writers use "he or she," which gets very old after about the one hundredth time.

EXAMPLE: "While an individual may think he or she likes chocolate, he or she hasn't seen *anything* until he or she has looked into the face of a menopausal woman who is holding a spatula, in which case he or she will quickly realize that he or she should not have eaten the last frozen Snickers bar, and now the entire question of 'he or she' is about to be emphatically answered."

Some writers have stooped to the awful construct of "s/he" to condense both "she" and "he" into a single new word. Just try reading that out loud at story time in the classroom.

But even if you are willing to resort to bad grammar or the jarring "s/he," you are still up against a whole raft of gender-specific words, unless you want to see "Take Your Chances" signs printed on the public rest room doors at the mall.

And I doubt you will soon see Hallmark greeting cards that read, "Congratulations on your bouncing baby human!"

And what about manhole covers? Do you want person-hole covers? Humanhole covers? Bipeds-with-the-ability-to reason-hole covers?

This is silly. People get *offended* so easily these days. There is nothing oppressive or sexist about the Declaration of Independence, the Lord's Prayer, or the English language. I think we all need to just lighten up a bit. For instance, even my mom, a former teacher, needs to stop being so defensive about her personal supply of Snapple and Snickers bars.

In fact, I think I'll just reach into the refrigerator here and . . .

WHACK, WHACK, WHACK!!!

OW, OW, OW!!!

Study Guide Questions

1. If you don't like English, you could take up French and move to Quebec and join the secession movement. As they used to say in Alabama, "Nothing succeeds like secession!" They thought this was quite humorous until General Grant showed up.

2. In order to promote inclusive language and break down stereotypical names, would you be willing to name your daughter "Fred" and your son "Sally"?

3. I suggest you listen to an old song by Johnny Cash titled "A Boy Named Sue" before you make any hasty decisions.

4. Let's say that your college kids get all hung up on this gender-neutral language stuff after being exposed to a bunch of whining liberal professors. When they are home on vacation and the phone rings for one of them, say to the caller, in a very loud voice, "Just a second and I'll get him or her for you." That will cure it.

5. God uses male imagery of himself quite a bit in the Old Testament, speaking of himself as the "husband" of the nation Israel, which is referred to as His "wife." Although feminist Bible critics often refer to God as "she," they never change the reference to Israel to make the nation the "husband." So we end up with the kind of imagery that spelled big trouble for the once bustling communities of Sodom and Gomorrah, where property values plummeted after all the real estate was summarily vaporized by fire from heaven. So a critic may want to think that over a bit before messing with God's revelation, unless s/he is looking for trouble.

Chapter 18

If You Can't Say Something Nice, You Still May Need to Say It

Jillions of mothers have warned jillions of children that if they can't say something nice, they should not say anything at all. The only problem with that advice is that it is wrong.

While we all want to raise children who are respectful and kind, we also want to train them to make distinctions between the good and the bad. If five-year-old Johnny observes that Uncle Ned is sure a grouch, the issue is not whether Johnny said something critical, but whether Uncle Ned is, indeed, a grouch—especially after he has sucked down half the bottle of Jack Daniels he hides under the seat of his car.

Remember that it was the young child who observed that the Emperor had no clothes. The adults were too wimpy to acknowledge the obvious.

We encourage our children to ask, "What would Jesus do?" while forgetting that Jesus routinely said rather harsh things like, "You brood of snakes! You hypocrites!" While He only said it when it was applicable, you can't escape the fact that His words were pretty tough at times.

Too often a child will make a factual observation about inappropriate adult behavior, only to be scolded for "not being nice."

Well, maybe Uncle Ned wouldn't be such a jerk if we all stopped pretending he wasn't.

I am not advocating unrestrained negative public comments from kids. Little Johnny can be taught not to blurt out all his observations at the dinner table. He can be taught that it is hurtful and rude to publicly comment on the weight of the person in the market check-out line, especially if the person is an author with a medically related donut impairment. But when Johnny is being tucked in at night and states, "I don't like Uncle Ned because he is mean," it is not fair to shush him and reply, "No, he isn't! And don't talk that way about your uncle!"

If Ned has a glaringly obvious drinking problem that turns him into a rude slob, what's wrong with acknowledging it?

"Johnny, you are right. We invite Uncle Ned over at Christmas because he is your daddy's brother and we care about him. We ask him not to drink alcohol before coming to our home, but sometimes he just ignores us and shows up acting like you just saw him. Uncle Ned drinks a lot of alcohol, and alcohol often makes people boorish and mean. That's why we don't let him stay long, and why Daddy takes his car keys and drives him home. That's also why we don't drink like Uncle Ned does. We sure don't want to be like that, do we?"

In addition to being a big fan of honesty, I am also a cheerleader for shame. I think shame can be great. I regret that there is so little of it today.

Not long ago, a member of a church choir in my town found herself expecting a baby. A bunch of other women in the choir were planning a big baby shower for her until a member of the pastoral staff squashed that idea like you would mash a cockroach scampering across the kitchen floor.

"This is not a cause for celebration," he said, throwing cold water on the baby shower. "She is pregnant out of wedlock, the father is married to someone else, she is behaving as though this is perfectly fine, she is unrepentant, and she ought to be ashamed of herself. If you want to buy her some baby stuff to help out, do so. But this is not something you celebrate with a party! We ought to be in mourning."

Preach it, brother!

There is a place for shame, especially when behavior is, well, shameful. All guilt is not bad guilt. Guilt is the sign of a functional conscience. Obviously, once people are sincerely repentant and have confessed their sins and sought forgiveness, we don't want them stuck in a pit of self-recrimination and guilt. God is a God who forgives if the forgiveness is sought sincerely and demonstrated by a change in behavior. But I think we simply *ignore* a lot of bad behavior, and indirectly *approve* it by failing to ever call a spade a spade. This helps no one, especially the person we are ostensibly being "nice" to.

Had the aforementioned pregnant woman been met with tears of grief instead of hugs when she announced her "blessed event," perhaps she would have been more easily persuaded to give the child up for adoption to a real home with a mom and a dad who could provide the kind of family setting God intended. This is not chauvinism. This is not mean-spirited condemnation. Look at the research. Children do best in a loving home with a mom and a dad. That's why God invented the family.

I am not saying we should ostracize single moms. To the contrary, we need to be as loving and kind as we possibly can be. But "loving and kind" does not mean we "affirm" every terrible decision and circumstance in the realm of human experience. Indeed, it was precisely because He was both loving and kind that Jesus was so tough on the Pharisees. Only by shocking them with the truth was there any possibility that they would stop embracing the lie that they were fine just the way they were.

Successful alcohol and drug recovery programs do not change people by ignoring the problems or excusing awful habits and behavior. They help precisely because brutal honesty is part of the package.

These programs are actually taking their cue from God, who insists on confession as a precursor to wholeness. This isn't about God rubbing our nose in our humiliating failures. This is not a divine "gotcha!" The whole shame and guilt and confession and repentance thing is about becoming healthy and free. It is about God being loving and kind, even if it feels like He is laying us open with a sword.

We don't like being cut with a knife. But in the hands of a physician who is ridding us of a malignant tumor, a knife can be the kindest cut of all.

One of the nicest things I ever did was yell at a friend who was about to torpedo his marriage.

It worked.

I could have just nodded sympathetically in order to be "nice," but *that* would have been a real shame.

Study Guide Questions

1. You may be saying to yourself, "Whoa! That was a pretty heavy chapter to stick in a humor book! That wasn't fair!"

2. Oh, stop complaining. It's like a tetanus shot. It may hurt, but it is for your own good.

3. You may also be saying, "There aren't even any questions here. Dave can't call this section 'Study Guide *Questions*' when there are no questions!"

4. Hey, life isn't fair. See chapter 38 for details.

Chapter 19

The Mysterious Man

The mysterious man moved into the house next door when I was about seven or eight years old. One of his hands was twisted and bent like a claw. He also walked with an awkward gait, as though one leg refused to share the burden of moving him. He rode a big tricycle around town, pedaling with his one good leg while his other leg just went along for the ride.

All the neighborhood kids immediately feared him. We would climb the tree in my backyard and spy on him through the bushes and try to reconstruct his history.

"Maybe he got shot robbing a bank!"

"Maybe he is a mad scientist!"

"Maybe his experiment blew up!"

The mysterious man could not have helped but notice that we ran for cover whenever he came outside, but he never said anything about it. This game of "hide-even-though-no-one-is-seeking" lasted for many weeks.

One day a group of us were out playing ball in the dead end street that ended at the driveway of the mysterious man, when he unexpectedly appeared in his doorway.

"Hey kids!" he called before we could even think of running. "Come on over. I'd like to show you something."

This invitation was extended back in the days before parents all warned their children never to speak to strangers, but we nevertheless all froze in place.

"C'mon," he called again, motioning us to his porch.

No one wanted to be the first one to bolt for home and thus endure the subsequent taunts of "Chicken!" So we moved in a tight group, like convicts chained together, up the sidewalk owned by the mysterious man.

"I suppose you kids are wondering how I got all banged up," he said.

(PAUSE FOR LONG AND UNCOMFORTABLE SILENCE.)

"We hadn't noticed," I finally said, while the herd nodded in agreement.

The mysterious man wrinkled his brow.

"You hadn't . . ." his voice trailed off.

"I never even saw the claw until now," said Scotty, as Dennis stomped on his foot to shut him up.

The man shook his head, and then smiled ever so slightly.

"Come on in," he said.

We squeezed through the door as a single huddled

mass yearning to breathe free, ready to make a run for it the split second he pulled out a monkey brain or electrodes or any of a hundred objects we conjectured he kept hidden in a secret back room.

We stood tensely in the living room while he opened the door to a small bedroom that was taken up with file cabinets and a desk.

He returned with a large envelope.

"I want to show you a few pictures," he said, sliding a stack of glossy black-and-white 8 x 10 photos onto the table.

"Cool!"

"Wow!"

"Righteous!"

There was a chorus of exclamations as we stared at the crisp photographs of a sleek U.S. Navy jet parked on the deck of an aircraft carrier. Next to the jet stood a younger version of the mysterious man—a version that was erect and proud and uncrippled.

Then he told us the story of long months at sea, a lashing storm, and a fateful flight. He spoke of heaving waves, the rise and fall of the carrier deck, the jarring crash, the flash of pain.

Quietly he set down a photo of the twisted metal that was once a multimillion-dollar fighter aircraft. It looked like a train had plowed into it.

"And that's how I ended up like this," he said.

There was a long pause before one of us cried out, "You're a hero!"

He just laughed.

We all ran home to tell our parents the great news that they no longer needed to fear the mysterious man, because he was a real live hero.

From that day forward we waved at the hero when he rode down the street on his huge tricycle. We brought other friends over to look at his photos. We made him tell the story over again to an expanding audience.

The wounds and injuries we once shunned took on an entirely new dimension once we understood the story behind the scars.

That is how the grotesque became noble.

That is how the ugly became heroic.

And that is how the cross became a crown.

Just as there were many who were appalled at him—
>   his appearance was so disfigured
>   beyond that of any man
>   and his form marred beyond human likeness—
so will he sprinkle many nations,
>   and kings will shut their mouths
>   because of him.
For what they were not told, they will see,
>   and what they have not heard they will
>   understand.
>   —Isaiah 52:14–15

Study Guide Questions

1. "Dave, do you regret that you never got around to telling your neighbor 'thank you' for his service to his country?"

   ANSWER: Yes. I regret it a lot. So to all you folks who have served, I want to extend a heartfelt "thank you." We all owe you.

2. Many people view Jesus as a heroic but tragic figure whose promising life as a moral teacher was cut short by an ignorant mob and brutal Roman officials. These people also think that the Christian faith is basically about living by the precepts laid down by this slain religious figure. What is wrong with this assessment of the Christian faith?

3. HINT: It has a lot to do with the fact that Jesus, unlike any other slain religious figure, rose from the dead. You can read all about it in the gospel of John in the New Testament. I highly recommend this.

Chapter 20

Church People

It seems that many church people fall into one of the following categories:

A. Nice, bubbly, biblically ignorant people
B. Peevish, haughty, theologically precise people

When they bump into each other at the annual potluck, the conversation goes like this:

Person A: "Praise the Lord! Let's hug!"

Person B: "If you don't use a Greek chain-reference lexicon, you are a slothful and mindless cretin."

Person A: "Praise the Lord! Let's hug!"

Obviously, that is a sweeping generalization. There are also other more nuanced categories consisting of:

C. Turtleneck wearing, ideological leftists who serve on missions committees that serve bourbon with soda, and where the mission consists of teaching indigenous peoples how to cook with solar ovens.

D. Earnest, well-meaning, guilt-laden people who are exhausted from serving on fourteen committees and writing letters to the editor.

Obviously, none of these categories is the ideal one in which to find yourself.

Our goal in this chapter is to study all these stereotypes and pick out key characteristics that we can "mix and match" to arrive at a balanced model consisting of: a bubbly, peevish, exhausted person who serves soda to indigenous peoples.

Hmmm. That's not quite right. Let's try that again.

What we want is a balanced model consisting of a slothful and mindless cretin who gives solar ovens to people in turtleneck sweaters.

That can't be right, either.

Boy, this is harder than I thought.

Let's break into our small groups and discuss.

Study Guide Questions

1. How come it seems like some of the most cocky people are those who have studied their Bible a lot and presumably know that it condemns arrogance?

2. Of course, the nice, bubbly ignorant ones can kind of get on your nerves.

3. "So, Mr. Big-Shot Author, what category are YOU in?"

4. I am in the special "Christian Writer" category, which means that I can actually be bubbly *about* being peevish. Do you find this unfair? Discuss.

5. Why do we have such a hard time engaging both the mind *and* the heart in living out our faith?

Chapter 21

The Uncivil War

The battle had been looming for weeks. My flight date had been set for well over a month, and Dale had been glumly marking off each day on the calendar.

"I'm going to miss you," she said.

"I'll miss you, too," I replied.

But a man's gotta do what a man's gotta do.

War is always so hard on the women who are left behind.

I kissed Dale good-bye and boarded the flight. Several hours later I touched down in Memphis, Tennessee. The weather was typical southern summer fare, and within moments my clothes were sticking to my back.

It was an unlikely group of guys who composed our unit. In civilian life, I was an aide to a member of Congress. Michael had just wrapped up a semester at the University of Tennessee, where he was engaged in some heavy-duty computer work for the Department of Defense. He would be tasked with recording the devastation on video-tape, which would be painstakingly analyzed again and again and again after the heat of battle was over.

Tim, our unit leader, worked as a substance-abuse counselor at a leading Memphis hospital. His colleagues had no clue about the double life he led.

Scott was a financial analyst for a British-owned company with a keen interest in penetrating the American market. He had been tasked with much of the acquisitions work. A not insignificant amount of money had been allotted to weaponry.

John was the wild card. With substantial training in hand-to-hand combat, his participation was critical, though he was harboring serious reservations about the operation. But he was in too deep to back out now—a fact that Tim reminded him of on more than one occasion.

By the following afternoon, the quiet suburban home that served as our command center would be a flurry of activity as plans were finalized and weapons were checked and rechecked.

Tim reviewed the staging area—three long boards laid across two saw horses—and nodded approvingly at the array of ammunition: a huge bowl of instant mashed potatoes (dyed green for added effect), two dozen partially melted chocolate fudge cookies, a massive vat of pork and beans, four dozen generic cans of soda, several twenty-four-ounce squeeze containers of French's yellow mustard—and that was just for starters.

Clearly, this would be the biggest food fight in Memphis history—and quite possibly the most heated battle the South had seen since the Union Army hammered Sherman's forces with the strategic but historically obscure surprise attack of lime Jell-O salad (with raisins).

Complicating the battle would be the presence of the mercenaries—numerous youngsters ranging from first-graders to high-schoolers. Their allegiance shifted on a minute-by-minute basis depending on which side produced the most interesting ammo.

"I think I'll just watch y'all have fun," said John, as Tim scooped two gallons of off-brand Neapolitan ice cream into a large pan, where it wilted under the fierce summer sun.

"I think you won't," Tim grinned in reply.

John's concern was quite understandable and quite warranted. The first food fight, conducted the prior summer, had been a far less lethal affair with only four participants and far more modest munitions. John's military training told him that this second battle would be a brutal, take-no-prisoners operation, where a likely key target would be the only retired member of the United States Marine Corps, who happened to be the father or grandfather of roughly half the assembled forces and who, hands down, presented the largest target available. A sixth sense told him that he would suffer massive collateral damage.

His premonition would be proved uncannily correct.

A seemingly inexhaustible supply of wickedly gooey groceries—foodstuffs that were never intended to share the same table, much less be hurled though the air at high speeds—were conveyed from the kitchen to the backyard, where the makeshift table groaned with the weight of it all.

Two dozen raw eggs floated in a green Tupperware bowl. A mess o' grits, left over from breakfast, provided an important statement about southern solidarity, and were apparently reserved for the poor schlep from California. (The author is convinced he was set up for the grits because he refused to eat them earlier.)

The ketchup, Cool Whip, bananas, and five-pound sack of Pillsbury unbleached flour filled out the basic ammo checklist. The six plastic bottles of root beer served as the food fighter version of weapons of mass destruction. With a small hole jabbed by an ice pick into the lid, the two-liter bottles (after a savage shaking) would emit an impressive stream of foaming fury that could reach a good fifteen feet.

The troops gathered merrily around the table amid John's stern warning to "LEAVE THE TABLE ALONE UNTIL THE 'BEFORE' PICTURE IS SNAPPED!" As the group of combatants smiled for the camera, they failed to notice John's massive paw reaching into the ice cream. The shutter clicked just in time to forever record the look of shocked surprise on Tim's face as a pint of frigid, multi-colored dessert began oozing down the inside of the back-side of his swim trunks.

Pandemonium erupted. The actual battle defies description. Imagine standing inside a gigantic food processor that is being fed by a deranged Julia Child and the image will be pretty close.

Grits spattered my face as I flung a glob of green potatoes in a retaliatory strike. A flurry of black-eyed peas pelted John as he peppered Scott with a particularly lethal barrage of diced peaches (in heavy syrup). John then slipped on a strategically placed banana and was immediately smothered by a generous representation of all the major food groups wielded by squealing, soda-drenched grandchildren.

The cold war doctrine of Mutual Assured Destruction was fully embraced by all sides. The air was a fog of hideously incompatible ingredients all randomly detonating on all targets.

There was no strategic defense, no "umbrella of protection" to ward off the incoming volleys of yams and globs of peach Jell-O. There was, however, a dizzying number of shifting alliances, double-crosses, and Machiavellian strategies—all formed and abandoned within seconds of what turned out to be a seven-minute war. Sort of like the State Legislature moments before it wraps up the final budget bills.

And the moral of the story is simply this: If you visit the South, you ain't leavin' until, one way or the other, you have tried some grits.

Study Guide Questions

1. "Dave, did this really happen?"

2. You bet your possum, it did. It was a hoot! I'd recommend it for special occasions like family reunions, youth group parties, small regional conflicts involving NATO, and to liven up the annual congregational business meeting.

3. "Dave, did your wife think this food fight was pathetic and infantile?"

4. Yes.

5. But I pointed out that while women bond through long and meaningful conversations, men bond by hurling groceries at each other. I explained that, really, these are just two sides of the same coin.

6. "And she accepted that?"

7. No. She thinks we are all semi-insane.

8. "Is this just one more example of your pointless, shallow, 'humor for humor's sake' chapters?"

9. Yep. But I make up for it in the next one.

Chapter 22

What Dave Would Tell You if He Was a Minister and You Accidentally Allowed Him into Your Pulpit One Day

As a kid my mental picture of God looked a lot like Judge Wapner. Kind of perturbed, short-tempered, and ready to bang down the gavel of judgment on a moment's notice.

In my mind, God perpetually had a clenched fist and muttered, "Why, I oughta just . . ."

I think early mental pictures we have of God can stick with us for decades, even if they are terribly incorrect images. So I lived a long time with the "Why, I oughta just . . ." view of God. Odds are, many of you have as well.

In fact, I am going to test you at this point. Ask yourself the following question. Answer it according to your gut-felt emotional response.

"When God thinks about me, what He *mostly* feels is . . ."

- Disappointment
- Sadness
- Wishes I would get my act together
- Wishes I was more faithful
- Delight
- Joy
- Elation that I am His child

I have been haunted for much of my life by the very question I have just asked you. How does God *feel* about me?

We often get it drilled into our heads that God *loves* us, but at the same time we often feel, in the recesses of our mind, that He doesn't particularly *like* us. It is as though loving us is in the job description that comes with being God—He does it, but it is almost obligatory. He loves us—in a disappointed, ticked-off sort of way.

I don't think that it is terribly surprising that we have this view of God. Based on a lot of what He said and did in the Old Testament, we can see that He was angry and disappointed in humanity, and even in His own chosen people, much of the time.

Look at the big introduction that the Israelites had when they met God at the Holy Mountain after Moses finally lead them out of Egypt. It is in the book of Exodus. Moses was invited up to the top to meet God, and all the people were warned not to even *touch* the mountain or they would die. God then shook the entire area with deafening thunder and flashes of lightning while smoke belched from the summit.

This did not move the congregation to break into a spontaneous chorus of "Yahweh loves me, this I know, for the Bible tells me so."

If I had been there I would have experienced an involuntary hygienic lapse right in my toga.

God's apparent intent was to communicate the following points:

1. "I am a Holy God."
2. "You are a sinful people."
3. "This is a problem."

He then went on to give Moses several hundred rules and regulations about how to perform ceremonies and sacrifices and generally patch things up with God when the people sinned. So while He was making a way by which they could get things right with Him, it was always at a distance. The Holy of Holies—the most sacred of all sites—was off limits to everyone but the high priest, and he only came in once a year and always with a sacrifice for his sins and for the sins of the nation.

"The Problem" was always staring them in the face.

Now, there were people like King David who really had a passion and a heart for God, and who literally took "delight" in the laws of God. But David had a barrier. Not even the king could approach God on the same basis as the high priest.

While the Old Testament is full of God's expression of commitment and loyalty and, yes, love to His people, that barrier always stood. He was always God-at-a-distance.

Then Jesus shows up. Christian theology teaches that Jesus always existed eternally as a member of the Godhead, one of the three persons who composes the Trinity, but that He entered our world at a given point in time as a baby. Actually, not as a baby. As a cell. God reduced himself to a cell, and lived and grew within the womb of a young Jewish virgin named Mary.

God incognito.

Which brings me to the passage of Scripture that has most changed my life in recent years. The passage that, more than any other, put all the pieces of the puzzle together.

I just flipped my Bible open one quiet morning when everyone else was gone, and I mulled over the fifth chapter of the gospel of Luke. It is the account of the day Jesus extended an invitation to a guy named Simon, subsequently named Peter.

The setting for this passage is very early in Jesus' ministry, before He has selected His disciples.

Peter is a professional fisherman by trade. He knows the sea, he knows the weather, and he knows fish. And he has just spent a night getting skunked. He has caught zero. So I don't imagine he is feeling too perky when Jesus shows up to preach to the people at the beach, where Peter is washing his nets. Peter is probably feeling kind of lousy. A whole night's work and nothing to show for it.

Peter is familiar with Jesus as a local rabbi who is an impressive teacher and who has a remarkable and clearly supernatural ability to heal diseases and illnesses. Indeed, Jesus had visited Peter's house and healed his mother-in-law, who was suffering from a high fever. So Peter is certainly going to listen to this amazing rabbi.

Here is the account:

> One day as Jesus was standing by the Lake of Gennesaret, with the people crowding around him and listening to the word of God, he saw at the water's edge two boats, left there by the fishermen, who were washing their nets. He got into one of the boats, the one belonging to Simon, and asked him to put out a little from shore. Then he sat down and taught the people from the boat.
>
> When he had finished speaking, he said to Simon, "Put out into deep water and let down the nets for a catch."
>
> Simon answered, "Master, we've worked hard all

night and haven't caught anything. But because you say so, I will let down the nets."

When they had done so, they caught such a large number of fish that their nets began to break. So they signaled their partners in the other boat to come and help them, and they came and filled both boats so full that they began to sink. (Luke 5:1–7)

Peter tosses out the net, and suddenly every fish in the lake is fighting to get into it. They are taking numbers and lining up. They are beating on the boat to get in. The perch are yelling at the bass for cutting in line. It is like nothing any fisherman has ever seen.

Now, you'd think Peter would be thrilled. You'd think he would call out, "I've got dibs on the rabbi! Hey, Jesus, how 'bout we start the 'Jesus and Simon Fishing Company, Inc.'? I'll do all the heavy lifting, and you just keep doing whatever it is you just did."

But that is not what Peter does.

"When Simon Peter saw this, he fell at Jesus' knees and said, 'Go away from me, Lord; I am a sinful man!' For he and all his companions were astonished at the catch of fish they had taken" (Luke 5:8–9).

He collapses at Jesus' knees and begs Him to leave.

"Go away from me," he pleads.

Go away. Please leave. Just leave me alone.

Why does he say that to the man who has just given him the best catch of his life?

Because Peter knew fish do not behave that way. He knew that he was in the presence of a miracle, and if he was in the presence of a miracle, he was in the presence of the Holy One. And the comparison between holiness and Peter was not a pretty picture. He was so scalded by his own guilt and failure and humiliating personal defeats that he collapsed at Jesus' feet and begged, "Go away from me, Lord; I am a sinful man!"

Go away. Please let me hide. It was just like Adam and Eve, running for the tall grass—like humanity has been running from God ever since.

When Peter said, "Go away from me, Lord," you need to understand that Peter was not rejecting Jesus. Peter was rejecting Peter.

Now, Jesus could have agreed with Peter. He could have said, "Yes, Simon, you are a sinful man! I hereby judge you and condemn you for your willful violations of God's law."

Jesus could have unloaded both barrels on Peter. He could have told him everything he had ever done. He could have emotionally obliterated Peter. And He would have been within His rights to do so. Peter really *was* a sinner—like we all are.

But He didn't condemn Peter. In fact, He didn't even discuss his sins. All He did was say, "Don't be afraid; from now on you will catch men."

"So they pulled their boats up on shore, left everything

and followed him" (Luke 5:10–11).

In today's words, Jesus was saying, "I want you on my team."

There was no clenched fist or backhanded threat from Jesus.

It isn't that Peter's sins and failures didn't matter—they did. Every lie, every cross word, every dark secret mattered. But Jesus already knew that He was going to take care of Peter's sin problem. Jesus was going to take Peter's sins, and yours, and mine, and destroy them at the cross. Peter didn't know it. At this point, he didn't have to. What mattered is that Jesus knew what He would do.

I believe that what Jesus said to Peter, He is saying as well to us: "Don't be afraid. I have not come to judge the world, but to save it. The son of man has come to seek and to save that which was lost.

"I want you on my team. I want you to join with me in spreading the good news about freedom, and a fresh start, and a God who so loved the world He gave His only son. Centuries of failure have shown that the old covenant—keeping the law—has not worked. The law does not liberate. But here is a new covenant. A new way. I will do for you what you cannot do for yourself. I will save you. It is all on me. Just trust me."

Peter was never the same.

If you, like Peter, take Jesus up on His offer to "follow

me," He is delighted beyond measure to have you on the team.

If you are living under a cloud of guilt, and if fear is keeping you from approaching God, you are living in the clutches of a diabolical lie. The Scripture tells us that "there is no fear in love, because perfect love casts out fear."

You cannot love what you fear.

Like He did with Peter, Jesus wants to release us from our fear by allowing us to understand the depth of God's love. This is not some sterile, distant love. This is passion. This is commitment. This is a thing of the heart.

This is love that departs from heaven, takes on the form of a man, pulls you to your feet, looks you in the eye, and says, "Do not fear. Believe in God. Believe also in me. I call you my friend."

But what about when we sin? I can hear you thinking.

Jesus addressed that very question in the story of the prodigal son. You remember the son who took his inheritance and went away on a life of sin.

Was the father grieved? Undoubtedly. Was he pained? Yes. But it was the grief and pain of love, not of rejection or rage.

And when the son turned to come home, here was the father's reaction:

"But while he was still a long way off, his father saw him and was filled with compassion for him; he ran to his son, threw his arms around him and kissed him" (Luke 15:20–22).

There is no clenched fist in that account. No recriminations. No anger. Just the love and forgiveness of a father for his erring child.

That is the mental picture Jesus wants us to have of God. Because the coming of Christ changed everything. The mountain no longer smokes. The veil that kept people out of the Holy of Holies was torn in half by God himself at the cross. We have been invited inside.

We have to become people of His Word instead of living in our flawed imaginations. We have to risk that the news that seems too good to be true is, in fact, true. Only by faith—wholehearted, abandoned faith—can we live truly free in mind, heart, and spirit.

I am going to end by answering for you the question I asked you earlier. If you have risked trusting God—or if you will, even now, at this moment, take Him at His Word, the following statement applies to you:

"When God thinks about me, what He *mostly* feels is . . ."

- Love
- Delight
- Joy
- Elation that you are His child
- And very, very, very pleased to have you on His team.

Study Guide Question

1. Do you ever take out some quiet time and just soak up a passage out of the Bible? I heartily recommend it. I think there is a somewhat mysterious enlightenment that happens during times like that. You have to actually try it to see what I mean.

Chapter 23

Grate Expectations

Let us now turn to the powerful, compelling tale of a married couple whom we shall refer to as "Carl and Mary"—mostly because those are their real names and this is a Christian book, so we are certainly not going to *lie* about their identities.

We believe in standards here at Bethany House Publishers, and if that means Carl and Mary happen to be scanning this chapter one day and are mortified to discover that their innermost marital trials and tribulations are plastered all over the page, and they stare at each other in shock and say, "How could Dave DO THIS to us?" I merely remind them that humility is a virtue. So really, this is for their own good. I think they should be grateful.

The tale begins back before Carl and Mary were dating, before they fell in love, before they said "I do" in front of God and the assembled witnesses, and *definitely* before the subsequent memorable moment when Carl, inexperienced young newlywed that he was, felt his pulse racing as he stared in slack-jawed wonder at their first VISA bill, and squawked, "You spent $489.27 for *clothes* in *one* day?"

And Mary burst into tears and said, "I just want to look nice for you!"

And Carl said, "But you already look great! You don't need all those clothes! In fact, the less clothes the better! Hey, that's an idea . . ."

And then he was in the mood for love, and she was in the mood to take a self-guided tour of Boise (and they lived in Sheboygan, so we aren't talking about a mere afternoon outing).

Clearly, it did not take long for the "great expectations" of marriage to become the "grate expectations" of reality. In the first twelve months of marriage, Carl and Mary were doing more grating than an industrial-sized cheese shredder.

Like all clueless young romantic people, Carl and Mary held certain expectations of what wedded bliss would be like *long* before anyone tossed rice at them. They came from very different family histories, with different socioeconomic levels, different spending habits, different temperaments, different understandings of what "normal life" was all about, and to top it all off they had *completely different genders*.

So it is not terribly surprising that they had wildly different expectations about married life. With all the afore-mentioned differences, one of the few things they actually had in common, going in, was that they at least came from the same continent.

It is at this point I would like to say that premarital counseling can fully resolve most of these differences and create harmony in the home. It is at this point that I would also like to hear Regis Philbin shout, "Congratulations, Dave! You are our newest millionaire!" But it is at this point that I also have to admit that neither of these things is likely.

Not that I am pooh-poohing premarital counseling. In fact, I think it is an outstanding idea. In our church, the pastoral staff will not marry a couple until they complete a prenuptial counseling course. I wish more churches would do this.

But even with some very open and informative counseling, where nitty-gritty issues like conflict resolution, budgets, in-laws, holidays, dirty socks he will leave by the bed, and various expectations are explored and discussed, these sessions only go so far because, deep down, she is lost in a romantic fog about the wedding ceremony and he is thinking about sex. So only about five or six words actually get through. That's why post-marriage counseling is a booming business.

Even if the engaged couple really does focus on the big issues, and even if they go into marriage with fairly realistic expectations about each other and general agreement about what roles they are going to be playing, the harsh reality is that men are men and women are women, and despite all the shrill rhetoric ever emitted by various feminist groups, there are profound differences between the genders, and these differences are deeper than who experiences water retention and terrible monthly mood swings.

EXAMPLE #1: My wife, Dale, and I were visiting my brother, Jim, and his wife, Beth, recently, and Beth used the term "adorable" about some little craft item she was showing my wife, and Dale agreed that it was, indeed, adorable, and they quickly scampered off to a store that sells cards and candles and little craft things, all of which they think are adorable.

Jim and I *never* used the word "adorable" the *entire* weekend we were together. We simply do not think in those terms. In fact, the same store that our wives could browse through for HOURS would put either of us in a coma after about fifteen minutes. That's why we are elated when they go to that store without us, even though it may very well mean some serious cardiac distress when the VISA bill comes.

EXAMPLE #2: When a woman is showing her husband an adorable little craft item she just purchased, and he is nodding when she asks if he thinks it would look good on a wall in their bedroom, the split second she says the word "bed" he is thinking about being in it.

They have different reactions and different expectations and different desires, not just because of backgrounds and families and economics, but because GOD MADE THEM THAT WAY.

But why?

My theory is—and I always get raised eyebrows when I say this—God is trying to manipulate us. But it is manipulation in a good way. He is trying to change us into something better than what we are. He wants us to grow—to learn to give and sacrifice and share and even suffer for the sake of someone else. And He knows that, if left to ourselves, we will not choose to do this. So He uses sex to get what He wants. Make no mistake, we guys would NOT be getting married if sex were not a big part of the package deal. We are *not* attracted to marriage because it increases our opportunity to view adorable craft items.

Hordes of words have already been penned about the different romantic expectations men and women hold, so I certainly do not need to dive into the subject yet again. But I am going to anyway. Hey, it's my book so I might just as well talk about something that interests me. If you don't like it, go get in line behind Carl and Mary.

Because I already said it so brilliantly in my previous book *Daze of Our Wives* (available at all Christian bookstores that have lowered their standards), I will quote myself here:

One common stereotype women have about men is that we are obsessed with sex. For example, just because [*Daze of Our Wives*] featured three chapters about sex, and because I tried to get away with two additional chapters about sex before my unamused editor began yelling at me, many women, such as my wife, are thinking, *Good grief! Is he obsessed with sex, or what?*

What an unfair stereotype! But even as women are unfairly caricaturing us guys as having the sex drive of hyperactive weasels, we men are quietly going about the daily business of doing our jobs, taking care of the lawn, paying bills, getting the tires rotated, and engaging in a host of other productive activities, in many cases going an *entire five minutes* without thinking about sex, which proves we are not obsessed with this topic, but merely very, interested in it. (That's "very" to the twenty-fourth power.)

Besides, for the record, the *Journal of the American Medical Association* has documented that men have the sex drive of hyperactive *ferrets*, not weasels. So there.

This high level of interest in sex is largely due to biological factors, and thus we guys could not change our colossal fascination with sex even if we wanted to, which we most certainly *don't*, because we really *like* being this way. It's fun! Just ask us! (If you happen to be married to us, that is!)

So we guys enter marriage with sex looming large in our minds. I am not saying that sex is not important for women as well. But let me illustrate the different expectations for intimacy.

EXAMPLE A: Carl and Mary have a nice evening out together at their favorite restaurant, and have arranged to have the kids spend the night with the grandparents. Carl and Mary have a chance to really talk, and they discuss their life, their faith, their hopes and dreams for their family—all over a fine dinner accented by soft candlelight and soothing music. Mary is fully prepared for a romantic interlude.

EXAMPLE B: Carl and Mary are watching the annual rerun of *The Ten Commandments* on TV. Carl is fully prepared for a romantic interlude between commercial breaks.

EXAMPLE C: Carl and Mary are just getting into bed when the radio, which is tuned to an "easy-listening station," interrupts with that irritating Emergency Broadcast System warning and the radio guy announces that the dam has burst and the city will be flooded within fifteen minutes. Carl says, "We still have time."

Clearly, with these radically different thresholds for intimate involvement, both Carl and Mary must learn to adapt to each other's needs and desires. In practical terms, he is going to have to learn to often s-l-o-w down and learn to proceed at a romantic pace that works for her.

Conversely, she needs to learn that in many cases he is going to be feeling way more amorous than she is, and she needs to learn to "speed up" to meet his needs and time constraints even though it is not going to be the same memorable experience outlined in Example A.

In short, they need to adapt to each other. And that adaptation spills into every facet of life.

He may think a dream vacation means elk hunting. She may think it means traveling to Chicago for a big family get-together. Obviously, these are mutually incompatible goals (unless the Windy City has seen a recent intrusion of large game animals).

It may be that they do one thing one year, and another thing the next. It may mean that he occasionally does a "solo" vacation, or goes off with a bunch of his hunting buddies. It may mean that they find a third alternative.

But it had better mean that they are talking and giving and working it out and putting each other first. Because no matter what expectations they brought into their union, they need to realize that God has His *own* expectations of marriage.

"Husbands, love your wives, just as Christ also loved the church and gave Himself up for her" (Ephesians 5:25 NASB).

Guys, Christ put the church, His "bride," first. He gave, and sacrificed, and willingly took death before He would allow harm to come to her. He put her *first*. And He expects us to put our wives first too.

And ladies, God has some expectations for you as well—expectations like "respectful behavior" and a "gentle and quiet spirit, which is precious in the sight of God" (1 Peter 3:2–4 NASB).

Talk about "great expectations!" These are HUGE expectations!

Clearly, putting others first does not mean "let them have or do whatever they want." Jesus does not let us have or do whatever we want. He puts us first by acting in our best interests. Many times, this means a firm but loving "no." Wisdom and sensitivity need to permeate all our decisions as married couples.

But there are lots of gray areas, when the issue is not a "yes or no" matter.

For instance, there is no single "correct" decision on how to spend the family income, or where to spend Christmas, or what car to buy (unless you are considering the same kind of lemon of a station wagon that I bought, in which case the answer is a resounding "no!").

But if husbands are truly loving their wives with the same fervor and sacrifice and commitment that Christ lavished on the church, then it should not be a huge stretch for wives to meet God's expectation for them to respect and love and accept the leadership of their mates.

I love to look at successful marriages that have made it forty or fifty years. Not that all long marriages are, by

definition, successful. There are long marriages that seem
more like a prison sentence than a blessed union. But
when I find an aging couple who are still crazy about each
other, who still date, who sit close together in church, and
who still kiss (not during the sermon), I spy on them so I
can learn something for my own marriage.

And what I am learning is that God does not intend
marriage to meet our expectations. He intends marriage to
exceed our wildest dreams.

Study Guide Questions

1. **QUESTION FOR MATURE MARRIED COUPLES:** "What are some of the differing expectations you brought into marriage? Would you be willing to share with an engaged couple the secrets you learned regarding how to resolve these issues?"

2. **QUESTION FOR ENGAGED PERSONS:** "Miss, can you put down that copy of *Bridal Shopping & Spending Extravaganza* magazine for just a moment while I direct your attention to the kind offer by an experienced married couple? Yes, I know the article about cummerbunds is fascinating, but if you could just focus for a moment on the big picture . . . Miss?"

   "OK, young engaged guy, since she is now absorbed in the article titled 'Choose the Right Cake Frosting or You'll RUIN the Most Important Day of Your Mortal Existence!' perhaps we can have a man-to-man talk about conflict resolution. Young man? Hello? Anyone home behind those glazed eyes? I'M TALKING TO YOU!!!"

3. Does this prove my point, or what?

Chapter 24

It All Depends

For weeks Scott had been contemplating what to get Marie for her fiftieth birthday. A thoughtful and loving husband, Scott was intent on diverting Marie's attention from the harsh reality that she was about to hit the half-century mark. He had already dropped several hints to let Marie know her gift would be something spectacular, and the excitement had the intended effect. Far from dreading the Big Five-O, Marie was almost giddy with anticipation.

Scott had narrowed the choices down to two: a dream vacation in either Hawaii or Italy. But he had not quite decided between the two.

"Soooooo? What are you going to get me for the big day?" Marie grinned one day as Scott pulled the car out of the driveway and onto the street.

"Depends," Scott mused, still weighing the merits of warm sandy beaches against the romantic charm of Tuscany.

Tragically, he mused just a tad too long.

Mistaking his one-word response for his final answer, Marie thought Scott had just offered to buy her an adult incontinence control product known by the brand name "Depends."

I won't go into detail about what happened next, other than to note that Marie's purse had to be surgically removed from Scott's spleen.

So what can we learn from this experience, aside from the interesting physics lesson that the speed of a purse increases exponentially as you multiply the length of the shoulder strap by the outrage quotient of the woman seated in the passenger seat?

Clearly, the lesson is that all guys should wear Kevlar vests that can stop a bazooka projectile. I mean, there is no way Scott could have seen that coming. It was a completely innocent mistake. He was utterly unaware that he had just delivered a pun of epic proportions. He was the hapless, oblivious victim of his own unintended mirth.

But let's suppose for a moment that Scott had, in fact, realized—just a split second before he uttered the word— that he was about to emit an extremely witty joke worthy of inclusion in a Jay Leno monologue. The overwhelming odds are that *he would have said it anyway*, truly clueless about (or at least grossly underestimating) the quick and blunt response it would elicit from his spouse. So whether it was purposeful or doltish, he was *destined** to utter that word and get whacked with a hyper-velocity handbag.

This tragic tale is compounded by the fact that—now listen up—Scott and Marie had both read a marriage book in past years, but this potentially explosive situation was *never* mentioned.

And that's the problem with most marriage books. They try to give you broad guidelines about how to behave in your marriage, but we don't live broadly. We live in a series of narrow, highly specific occasions that may never again arise. That's why I plan to write a marriage counseling book someday. You've probably already perused a wad of generalized material about communication, conflict resolution, expectations, and tips to keep romance alive. But what you really need is a book that explains the commonly overlooked, unique marriage topics; such as why your wife will get all bent out of shape if you try to rebuild a 1967 Pontiac engine in the bathroom *even after* you explain that you need a "clean room" for the final assembly.

(Yes, I am personally acquainted with a guy who rebuilt an engine in a bathroom. In all fairness to him, if women can have those fancy little sculpted soaps by the bathroom sink, why shouldn't guys be able to have a couple of GTO pistons draped artfully across the toilet tank?)

---

*This is what theologians mean when they talk about "personal responsibility" and "predestination" being simultaneously true.

But how many marriage books have ever raised this *specific* issue as a potential source of marital conflict? Zero, that's how many. That's why I am planning to run to the rescue with an alternative, cutting-edge marriage manual chock-full of material that just may happen to address perhaps one of the situations that could possibly arise in your nuptial relationship.

Then again, maybe not. I mean, I can't possibly cover every bizarre episode you people come up with. So you may have to generalize some kind of moral point from what you read, such as the obvious lesson from Scott and Marie, which is: "Never Say *Anything* That Could Be Misunderstood."

I have oodles of great tips like that. Here's another one:

"If you buy stocks low and sell high, you could make tons of loot."

I can shovel out helpful advice by the cubic yard. All you have to do is act upon these tips and you will never be misunderstood, plus you will be rich enough to buy Jamaica and crown yourself emperor for life.

Wow! That sounds pretty good. Maybe I'll just take my own advice before you do and then put dibs on the best beach. Plus, if I am royalty, maybe my family will hold me in awe instead of making fun of my bald spot. Let's jump to the Study Guide Questions to explore this further.

Study Guide Questions

1. If I became Emperor of Jamaica, I wonder if I could get someone else to pick up my socks by the side of the bed?

   (PAUSE FOR MISUNDERSTANDING TO ENSUE.)

2. "What's that, Brad? What do you mean, 'How did'ja make her pick up your socks?' Make WHO pick up my socks?"

   (PAUSE FOR SNOWBALL EFFECT.)

3. "That's JAMAICA not 'Ja make her!'"

   (PAUSE FOR AVALANCHE EFFECT.)

4. "Dale, notwithstanding anything Brad told you, I did NOT say I could MAKE you pick up my socks! Who are you going to believe, your clearly demented son or the Emperor for Life?"

5. Well, folks, it looks like we are doomed to have misunderstandings after all. So plan on explaining and apologizing a lot. Dinner out helps too. And always, always, always pick up your own socks.